Nǐ hǎo

Just Enough **Chinese**

D.L. Ellis

Beth McKillop

Guo Jin

Jin Hong

PASSPORT BOOKS
a division of *NTC Publishing Group*
Lincolnwood, Illinois USA

1993 Printing

This edition first published in 1991 by Passport Books, a division of
NTC Publishing Group, 4255 West Touhy Avenue, Lincolnwood
(Chicago), Illinois 60645-1975 U.S.A.
Originally published by Pan Books. © D. L. Ellis and Beth McKillop,
1990.
Manufactured in the United States of America.

3 4 5 6 7 8 9 AG 9 8 7 6 5 4 3 2

Contents

Using the phrase book

- This phrase book is designed to help you get by in China, to get what you want or need. It concentrates on the simplest but most effective way you can express these needs in an unfamiliar language.
- The **Contents** on page 5 gives you a good idea of which section to consult for the phrase you need.
- The **Index** on page 155 gives more detailed information about where to look for your phrase.
- When you have found the right page you will be given:
  either – the exact phrase
  or   – help in making up a suitable sentence
  and   – help in getting the pronunciation right.
- The English sentences in **bold type** will be useful for you in a variety of different situations, so they are worth learning by heart.
  (See also **DO IT YOURSELF**, page 148)
- Wherever possible you will find help in understanding what Chinese people are saying to you in reply to your questions.
- If you want to practise the basic nuts and bolts of the language further, look at the **DO IT YOURSELF** section starting on page 148.
- Note especially these three sections:
  Everyday expressions, page 14
  Shop talk, page 60
  Sign language, page 125
  You are sure to want to refer to them most frequently.
- Once in China, remember to use the local tourist offices (see page 29).

North American Addresses:
China National Tourist Office
Lincoln Building
#3126, 60 East 42nd Street
New York, NY 10165
Tel: (212) 867-0271

China National Tourist Office
333 West Broadway
Suite 201
Glendale, CA 91204
Tel: (818) 545-7505/7

A note on the pronunciation system

It is usual in phrase books for there to be a pronunciation section, which tries to teach English-speaking tourists how to pronounce correctly the language of the country they are visiting. Such attempts are based on the argument that correct pronunciation is essential for comprehension. The system in this book, however, is founded on three quite different assumptions: firstly, that it is not possible to describe in print the sounds of a foreign language in such a way that the English speaker with no phonetic training will produce them accurately, or even intelligibly; secondly, that perfect pronunciation is not essential for communication; and lastly, that the average visitor abroad is more interested in achieving successful communication than in learning how to pronounce new speech sounds. Observation and experience have shown these assumptions to be justified. The most important characteristic of the present system, therefore, is that it makes no attempt whatsoever to teach the sounds of the other language, but uses instead the nearest English sounds to them. The sentences transcribed for pronunciation are designed to be read as naturally as possible, as if they were ordinary English (of a generally South-Eastern English variety), and with no attempt to make the words sound 'foreign'. In this way you will still sound quite English, but you will at the same time be understood. Practice always helps performance, and it is a good idea to rehearse aloud any of the sentences you know you are going to need. When you do come to the point of using them, say them with conviction.

- Dozens of different dialects of Chinese are spoken throughout the country. This book describes the sounds of the kind of Chinese spoken in north China, around Peking, which is taught in schools and broadcast throughout China. You will certainly notice differences in the way people speak, particularly between north and south China, but almost everywhere you will find young people who know enough standard Chinese to make communication possible.
- Chinese characters – the written language – are common to all parts of China and can be understood by speakers of all the dialects, and you can make yourself understood by pointing to the Chinese characters beside the phrase you are saying.
- Don't be daunted by the reputation of Chinese as a difficult

language. Speaking Chinese is surprisingly easy: you don't have to remember past present and future for verbs and you don't have to bother with singular and plural for nouns. You may think that because Chinese is a tonal language, you will never make yourself understood. It's true that the same sound pronounced in two different tones has two different meanings: yān is tobacco, yán is salt – táng is sugar, tāng is soup. However, most speech does not consist of single syllables and most of what you say will be supplied by context. Remember that Chinese people from the south and west of the country speak completely differently from northerners, and yet they all manage to make themselves understood. It's more important to stress what you say convincingly and forget about tones, until you are put right by your Chinese hosts.

The four tones at a glance

The four tones in Peking dialect are represented by (1), (2), (3) and (4) in the following figure:

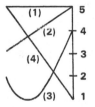

The 1st tone is a 'high-level' tone. In writing it is represented by the pitch-graph '¯' e.g. 'gū', 'bā'.

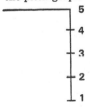

The 2nd tone is a 'high-rising' tone. It is represented by the pitch-graph ''', e.g. 'dá', 'gé'.

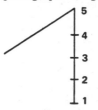

The 3rd tone is a 'falling-and rising' tone. It descends from mid-low to low pitch and then rises to a mid-high pitch. It is represented by the pitch-graph '˘', e.g. 'bǎ' and 'nǚ'.

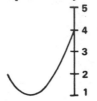

The 4th tone is a 'falling' tone, it falls from high to low. The pitch-graph is '`', e.g. 'tù' and 'pò'.

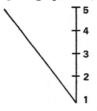

Some syllables are 'light or 'tone-less'. In these cases, no pitch-graph sign is shown above the vowel, e.g. the question indicator 'ma'.

- Because Chinese is written with characters, speakers of languages written alphabetically have an extra difficulty in reading the language.
- In this book, we have laid out the Chinese versions of the phrases you will be using like this

I want to make a phonecall   **Wǒ xiǎng dǎ diànhuà**
Waw syang da dyenn-hwa
我想打电话

For people who have learned Chinese formally, pinyin, the first of the two versions in the right-hand column, will give you an exact guide to pronunciation. The tones of Chinese are also indicated, above each syllable. Where no tone mark is given, the syllable should be pronounced lightly, without emphasis.
- After pinyin comes an anglicized rendering of the Chinese words: just pronouce the sounds as you would English, and you will come fairly close to pronouncing Chinese.
- Finally, the Chinese characters are given, in the simplified form used in China proper, so that you can point to them if you get into difficulties.
  Pinyin is an invented alphabet, used in China to teach the sounds of the Chinese language. Once learned, it never varies, unlike English, where the letter 'a' can represent several different sounds for example. The only way to learn the sounds correctly is to listen and practise. Buy a cassette tape of standard Chinese for beginners and practise before travelling in China: the BBC's *Get by in Chinese* is a good starting point. (BBC Books, 1988).
- The main differences between English readings and pinyin readings of the letters of the alphabet are:

Letter	Pinyin reading
c	ts like nuts
z	dz like fads
h	like a German or Scottish ch
	ich loch
x	half way between s and sh
zh	like the j in jar

The China Guidebook (Macmillan) is updated annually. This is designed with group travellers in mind.

Visit travel offices either in the U.S. or in Hong Kong before getting to China, since availability of maps, timetables and general information about travel varies enormously from place to place inside China.

China's administrative divisions and provincial/regional capitals

Everyday expressions

[*See also 'Shop talk', p.14*]

Hello (to one person)	**Nǐ hǎo** Nee how 你好
(to more than one person)	**Nǐmen hǎo** Nee-min how 你们好
Goodbye	**Zài jiàn** Dzay jenn 再见
Yes	**Shì** Shir 是
Please	**Qǐng** Cheeng 请
Great	**Hǎo** How 好
Thank you	**Xièxiè** Sie-sie 谢谢
That's right	**Duìle** Dway-la 对了
Yes	**Shì (yes it is)** Shir 是 **Yǒu (yes there is)** Yoh 有
No	**Bù** Boo 不
No thanks	**Xièxie,bù yào** Sie-sie, boo yow 谢谢不要

I disagree	**Wǒ bù tóngyì** Waw boo toong-ee 我不同意
Excuse me	**Láojià** Low-jya 劳驾
Sorry	**Duìbuqǐ** Dway-boo-chee 对不起
Don't mention it	**Bù kèqi** Boo ker-chee 不客气
That's good	**Hěn hǎo** Hinn how 很好
That's no good	**Bu hao** Boo how 不好
I know	**Wǒ zhīdao** Waw jir-dow 我知道
I don't know	**Wǒ bù zhīdao** Waw boo jir-dow 我不知道
It doesn't matter	**Méiyǒu guānxi** May-yow gwan-see 没有关系
Where's the toilet please?	**Qǐngwèn, cèsuǒ zài nǎr?** Cheeng-win, tse-swor dzigh narr 请问，厕所在哪儿？
How much is that? *(point)*	**Duōshǎo qián?** Daw-show chyen 多少钱
Is service included?	**Bāokuò fúwùfèi ma?** Bow-kwo foo-woo-fay ma 包括服务费吗？
Do you speak English?	**Nǐ huì Yīngwén ma?** Nee whey Eeng-win ma 你会英文吗？
I'm sorry	**Hěn bàoqiàn** Hinn bow-chyenn 很抱歉

I don't speak Chinese	**Wǒ bù huì Zhōngwén** Waw boo whey Joong-win 我不会中文
I only speak a little Chinese	**Huì yīdiǎn Zhōngwén** Whey ee dyenn Joong-win 会一点中文
I don't understand	**Wǒ bù dǒng** Waw boo doong 我不懂
Please, can you ...	**Qǐng nǐ ...** Cheeng nee ... 请你...
repeat that?	**zài shuō yī biàn?** dzigh shaw ee byenn 再说一边?
speak more slowly?	**shuō màn diàn?** shaw man dyenn 说慢点?
write it down?	**xiě?** sye 写?
What is this called in Chinese? *(point)*	**Zhèige Zhōngwén jiào shémme?** Jay-ge Joong-win jow shum-ma 这个中文叫什么?

Crossing the border

ESSENTIAL INFORMATION

- Most people travel to China by plane; some will enter by train (from Hong Kong or on the Mongolian or Russian border) or by boat. Car drivers can visit from Hong Kong or Macao, and will have to be ready for the slow speeds and undisciplined traffic on most Chinese roads.
- At the customs point, you will be asked to declare electronic goods, jewellery and non-Chinese currency. Your foreign currency will be exchanged for FECs (Foreign Exchange Certificates).

- You should keep records of currency you exchange in China in case you need to change FECs back into foreign currency on leaving the country. It is forbidden to export Chinese currency, except for small amounts as a souvenir.
- You will need a valid visa to enter China. This can be obtained either through China International Travel Service, a Chinese Embassy Consular Section, or at Beijing airport on arrival. Most customs officials will speak some English. It is useful to know Shì 'yes it is' and Yǒu 'yes I have', bùshì 'no it isn't' and méiyǒu 'no I haven't'.

ROUTINE QUESTIONS

Passport?	**Hùzhào** Hoo-jow 护照
Insurance?	**Bǎoxiǎn** Bow-syenn 保险
Registration	**Zhùcè** Jew-tsuh 注册
Plane ticket	**Fēijīpiào** Fay-jee-pyow 飞机票
Train ticket	**Chēpiào** Chuh-pyow 车票
Goods to declare	**Shēnbào** Shinn-bow 申报
Where are you going?	**Dào nǎr qù?** Dow narr chew 到哪儿去?
How long are you staying?	**Dāi duō jiǔ?** Dai daw jew 呆多久?
Where have you come from?	**Nǎr lái de?** Narr lye di 哪儿来的?
Visa and entry forms may require: surname	**xìng** seeng 姓

first name	**míngzi** ming-dz 名子
date of birth	**chūshēng rìqī** choo-shung ri-chee 出生日期
place of birth	**chūshēng dì** choo-shung dee 出生地
address	**dìzhǐ** dee-jih 地址
nationality	**guójí** gwo-jee 国籍
profession	**zhíyè** jih-ye 职业
passport number	**hùzhào hàomǎ** hoo-jow how-ma 护照号码
issued at ...	**yú...fā** yoo...far 于...发
signature	**qiānzì** chyenn-z 签字

Meeting people

[*See also 'Everyday expressions', p.18*]

Breaking the ice

Hello Good morning How are you?	**Nǐ hǎo** Nee how 你好 Nín hao is more polite 您好 Nǐmen hǎo (Neemen how) 你们好 is used when addressing more than one person

Pleased to meet you	**Gāoxìng rènshi nín** Gow-seeng rinn-shir neen 高兴认识您
I am in China for ...	**Wǒ lái Zhōngguó wèile ...** Waw ligh Joong-gwo way-la ... 我来中国为了...
holidays	**lǔxíng** loo-sing 旅行
business	**zuò shēngyì** dzo shung-ee 做生意
Can I offer you ...	**Nín xiǎng yào** Neen syang yow 您想要
a drink	**hē shénme** her shumma 喝什么
a cigarette	**chōu yān ma** choe yenn ma 抽烟吗
Are you staying long?	**Nǐ dāi hěn cháng shíjiān ma?** Nee digh hinn chang shi-jenn ma 你呆很长时间吗?
Name What's your name?	**Nín guìxìng?** Neen gway-seeng 您贵姓?
My name is ...	**Wǒ xìng ...** Waw seeng ... 我姓
Family Are you married?	**Jiéhūnle ma?** Jyeh-hoon-la ma 结婚了吗?
I am married	**Jiéhūnle** Jyeh-hoon-la 结婚了
I am single	**Méi jiéhūn** May jyeh-hoon 没结婚
This is ...	**Zhèiwèi shì ...** Jay-way shi ... 这位是..

my wife	**wǒ qīzi** waw chee-dz 我妻子
my husband	**wǒ zhàngfu** waw jang-foo 我丈夫
my son	**wǒ érzi** waw urr-dz 我儿子
my daughter	**wǒ nǚ'ér** waw noo-urr 我女儿
my boyfriend/girlfriend	**wǒ péngyou** waw pung-yow 我朋友
my colleague	**wǒ tóngshì** waw toong-shi 我同事
Do you have any children?	**Yǒu háizi ma?** Yow high-dz ma 有孩子吗?
I have ...	**You ...** Yow ... 有
one daughter	**yīge nǚ'ér** ee-ga noo-urr 一个女儿
one son	**yīge érzi** ee-ga urr-dz 一个儿子
two daughters	**liǎngge nǚ'ér** lyang-ga noo-urr 两个女儿
three sons	**sānge érzi** san-ga urr-dz 三个儿子
No, I haven't any children	**Méi háizi** May high-dz 没孩子
Where you live **Are you ...**	**Nǐ shì ...** If plural, **Nǐmen shì** Nee shi ... (Nee-men shi) 你是...(你们是...)

Chinese?	**Zhōngguó rén ma?**
	Joong-gwo rin ma
	中国人吗?
from Hong Kong?	**Xiānggǎng rén ma?**
	Syang-gang rin ma
	香港人吗?
Taiwanese?	**Táiwān rén ma?**
	Tai-wan rin ma
	台湾人吗?
Japanese?	**Rìběn rén ma?**
	Ri-bin rin ma
	日本人吗?
Singaporean?	**Xīnjiāpō rén ma?**
	Seen-jya-po rin ma
	新加坡人吗?
I am ...	**Wǒ shì ...**
	Waw shir ...
	我是
American	**Měiguó rén**
	May-gwo rin
	美国人
English	**Yīngguó rén**
	Yeeng-gwo rin
	英国人

[For other nationalities, see p.142]

I live ...	**Wǒ zhù ...**
	Waw jew ...
	我住
in London	**Lúndūn**
	Loon-doon
	伦敦
in England	**Yīngguó**
	Eeng-gwo
	英国
in the north	**běifāng**
	bay-fang
	北方
in the south	**nánfāng**
	nan-fang
	南方

in the east	**dōngfáng** dong-fang 东方
in the west	**xīfáng** see-fang 西方
in the centre	**zhōngbù** joong-boo 中部
in a big city	**zài dà chéngshì** dzigh da chung-shir 在大城市
in the countryside	**zài nóngcūn** dzigh noong tsoon 在农村

For the businessman and woman

I'm from ... *(firm's name)*	**Wǒ dàibiǎo ...** Wo digh-byaow ... 我代表...
I have an appointment with ...	**Wǒ gēn ... yuēhǎole** Waw gin ... ywe-haow la 我跟...约好了
May I speak to ...	**Néng gēn ... shuōhuà ma?** Nung gen ... shwo-hwa ma 能跟....说话吗?
This is my card	**Zhèi shì míngpiàn** Jay shi meeng-pyenn 这是名片
I'm sorry, I'm late	**Hěn bàoqiàn, láiwǎnle** Hin baow-chyenn, ligh-wan-la 很抱歉，来晚了
Can I fix another appointment?	**Néng zài yuē shíjiān ma?** Nung dzigh ywe shijyenn ma 能再约时间吗?
I'm staying at the (Friendship) hotel	**Wǒ zhù (Yǒuyì) Fàndiàn** Waw jew (Yow-ee) Fan-dyenn 我住（友谊）饭店
I'm staying in (Nanjing) Road	**Wǒ zhù (Nánjīng) Lù** Waw jew (Nan-jeeng) Loo 我住（南京）路

Asking the way

ESSENTIAL INFORMATION

WHAT TO SAY

Excuse me, please	**Qǐngwèn** Cheeng-win 请问
How do I get ...	**Dào ... zěnme zǒu?** Dow ... dzumma dzow 到...怎么走?
to Shanghai?	**Shànghǎi** 上海
to Nanjing Road?	**Nánjīng lù** Nan-jeeng loo 南京路
to the hotel?	**bīnguǎn** been-gwan 宾馆
to the beach?	**hǎibīn** high-been 海滨
to the bus station?	**qìchē zhàn** chee-chuh jann 汽车站
to the historic site?	**míngshèng gǔjì** ming-shung goo-jee 名胜古迹
to the market?	**shìchǎng** shir-chang 市场
to the police station?	**jǐngchá jú** jing-cha joo 警察局
to the port?	**gǎngkǒu** gang-kow 港口
to the post office?	**yóujú** yow-ju 邮局

to the railway station?	**huǒchē zhàn** hwo-chur jann 火车站
to the sports stadium?	**tǐyù guǎn** tee-yoo gwann 体育馆
to the tourist office?	**lǔxíng shè** loo-sing shur 旅行社
to the town centre?	**chénglǐ** chung-lee 城里
to the town hall?	**zhèngfǔ bàngōnglóu** jung-foo ban-goong-low 政府办公楼
Is there a ... near here?	**Zhèr fùjìn yǒu ... ma?** Jurr foo-jeen yow ... ma 这儿附近有...吗?
art gallery	**měishù guǎn** may-shoo gwann 美术馆
baker's shop	**miànbāo diàn** mien-baow dyenn 面包店
bank	**yínháng** yeen-hang 银行
bar	**jiǔguǎn** jew-gwann 酒馆
botanic garden	**zhíwù yuán** jir-woo ywann 植物园
bus stop	**qìchē zhàn** chee-chuh jann 汽车站
butcher's shop	**shēngròu diàn** shung-row dyenn 生肉店
café	**xiǎochī bù** siow-chir boo 小吃部
cake shop	**diǎnxīn bù** dyenn-seen boo 点心部

campsite	**yíngdì** yeeng-dee 营地
bureau de change	**huànqián de dìfang** hwan-chyenn di dee-fang 换钱的地方
chemist shop	**yàodiàn** yaow-dyenn 药店
church	**jiàotáng** jyaow-tang 教堂
cinema	**diànyǐng yuàn** dyenn-yeeng ywann 电影院
delicatessen	**shúshí bù** shoo-shir boo 熟食部
dentist	**yáyī** ya-yee 牙医
department store	**bǎihuò shāngdiàn** bye-hwo shang-dyenn 百货商店
disco	**dísīkē** dee-sir-ko 迪斯科
doctor	**yīshēng/dàifu** yee-sheng/digh-foo 医生／大夫
fishmonger	**mài yǔde** my yoo-dee 卖鱼的
Friendship Store	**Yǒuyì Shāngdiàn** Yow-ee Shang-dyenn 友谊商店
garage	**chēkù** chuh-koo 车库
greengrocer	**shūcài shǔiguǒ shāngdiàn** shoo-tsigh shway-gwo shang-dyenn 蔬菜水果商店

grocer	**záhuò shāngdiàn** dza-hwo shang-dyenn 杂货商店
hairdresser	**lǐfà diàn** lee-fa dyenn 理发店
hardware shop	**rìyòngpǐn shāngdiàn** ri-yoong-pin shang-dyenn 日用品商店
hospital	**yīyuàn** yee-ywann 医院
hostel (cheap hotel)	**lǚdiàn** loo-dyenn 旅店

[NB: Youth hostels do not exist in China, but students can find dormitory or cheap accommodation by insisting they can't pay the full rate. Take and show a student card.]

hotel	**lǚguǎn/bīnguǎn** loo-gwann/bin-gwann 旅馆／宾馆
ice-cream parlour	**bīngqílín diàn** bing-chee-lin dyenn 冰淇淋店
laundry	**xǐ-yī diàn** see-ee dyenn 洗衣店
museum	**bówùguǎn** bo-woo gwann 博物馆
newsagent	**mài bàozhǐde** my baow-jir-di 卖报纸的
night-club	**yèzǒnghuì** ye-dzoong-hway 夜总会
park	**gōngyuán** goong-ywann 公园
petrol station	**jiāyóu zhàn** jya-yow jann 加油站

postbox	**xìnxiāng**
	seen-syang
	信箱
public toilet	**gōnggòng cèsuǒ**
	goong-goong tser-saw
	公共厕所
restaurant	**fàndiàn**
	fan-dyenn
	饭店
snack bar	**xiǎochībù**
	syow-chir-boo
	小吃部
sports ground	**tǐyùguǎn**
	tee-yoo-gwann
	体育馆
supermarket	**chāojí shìchǎng**
	chow-jee shir-chang
	超级市场
sweet shop	**tángguǒ diàn**
	tang-gwo dyenn
	糖果店
swimming pool	**yóuyǒng chí**
	yow-yoong chi
	游泳池
taxi stand	**chūzū qìchē zhàn**
	choo-zoo chee-chuh jann
	出租汽车站
telephone	**diànhuà**
	dyenn-hwa
	电话
theatre	**jùchǎng**
	joo-chang
	剧场
tobacconist	**yāncǎodiàn**
	yen-tsao-dyenn
	烟草店
travel agent	**lǚxíng shè**
	loo-sing sheh
	旅行社
zoo	**dòngwùyuán**
	doong-woo-ywann
	动物园

DIRECTIONS

- Asking where a place is or if a place is nearby is one thing: making sense of the answer is another.

Left/Right	**Zuǒ/Yòu** Dzo/Yow 左/右
Straight on	**yìzhí** ee-jih 一直
There	**Nàr** Narr 那儿
First left/ right	**Dào dìyī ge lùkǒu, wàng zuǒ/ yòu guǎi** Daow dee-yee ga loo-kow, wang dzo/yow gwigh 到第一个路口，往左/右拐
Second left/right	**Dào dìèr ge lùkǒu, wàng zuǒ/ yòu guǎi** Daow dee-urr ga loo-kow, wang dzo/yow gwigh 到第二个路口，往左/右拐
At the crossroads	**Dào lùkǒu** Daow loo-kow 到路口
At the traffic lights	**Dào hónglǜ dēng** Daow hoong-loo dung 到红绿灯
At the roundabout	**Dào huándǎo** Daow hwann-daow 到玩岛
At the level crossing	**Zài píng jiāodào** Dzigh ping jyaow-daow 在平交道
It's near/ far	**Hěn jìn/Hěn yuǎn** Hinn jeen/ Hinn ywann 很近/很远
One kilometre	**Yī gōnglǐ** Ee goong-lee 一公里
Two kilometres	**Liǎng gōnglǐ** Lyang goong-lee 两公里

Five minutes ...	**Wǔ fēn zhōng** Woo fin joong 五分钟
on foot/by car	**zǒulù/ kāichē** dzow-loo/kigh-chuh 走路／开车
Take ...	**Zuò ...** Dzo ... 坐...
the bus	**gōnggòng qìchē** goong-goong chee-chuh 公共汽车
the train	**huǒchē** hwo-chuh 火车
the trolley-bus	**wúguǐ diànchē** woo-gway dyenn-chuh 无轨电车
the underground	**dìtiě** dee-tyeh
[*For public transport, see p.114*]	地铁

The tourist information office

ESSENTIAL INFORMATION

- Written and verbal information is available in most large hotels and in the offices of Luxingshe or China International Travel Service (CITS). Maps and timetables are infuriatingly hard to come by in some Chinese cities, so stock up in Hong Kong or through your travel agent before setting out: a great deal of useful information can also be found in standard guidebooks (see pages 7, 11 and 154).
- CITS can also advise you about which cities are 'open' and which require permits (lǚyóu zhèng/ loo-yow jung) and about where to apply for these (the public security office).
- If you are travelling independently, you should check local practice about buying tickets through CITS. It is sometimes possible to avoid foreigners' surcharges by buying tickets directly at stations, ports and airports.

- The standard of information available through CITS guides is extremely variable, and journey times are very much longer than most western travellers are used to (36 hours Beijing-Canton by train, three and a half days from Shanghai to Urumqi) so it is only sensible to do some reading and planning before travelling to China.
  * Look for this sign 旅行社 LǓXÍNG SHÈ

WHAT TO SAY

Please have you got ...	**Nǐmen yǒu méiyǒu ...** Nee-min yow-may-yow ... 你们有没有...
a plan of the town?	**shì dìtú?** shih dee-too 市地图？
a list of hotels?	**lǚguǎn míngdān?** loo-gwann ming-dan 旅馆名单？
a list of coach excursions?	**yóulǎnchē shíkèbiǎo?** yow-lan-chuh shir-ko-byaow 游览车时刻表？
a leaflet on the town?	**běnchéng jièshào shū?** bin-chung jye-show shoo 本城介绍书？
a leaflet on the region?	**dìfāng jièshào shū?** dee-fang jye-show shoo 地方介绍书？
Please have you got ...	**Qǐng gěi wǒ yīge ...** Cheeng gay waw ee-ga ... 请给我一个...
a railway timetable?	**huǒchē shíkèbiǎo?** hwo-chuh shih-ko-byow 火车时刻表？
a bus timetable?	**gōnggòng qìchē shíkèbiǎo?** goong-goong chee-chuh shih-ko-byow 公共汽车时刻表？
In English, please	**Yào Yīngwénde** Yow Yeeng-win-di 要英文的
How much do I owe you?	**Duōshǎo qián?** Daw-shou chyenn 多少钱？

Can you recommend ...	**Néng jièshào yīge ...**
	Nung jye-shou ee-ga ...
	能介绍一个....
a cheap hotel?	**piányīdiǎn de fàndiàn?**
	pyenn-ee-dienn de fan-dienn
	便宜点的饭店 ?
a cheap restaurant?	**piányīde cānguǎn?**
	pyenn-ee de tsan-gwann
	便宜的餐馆?
Can you make the booking for me?	**Néng gěi wǒ dìng piào ma?**
	Nung gay waw ding piaow ma
	能给我订票吗?

LIKELY ANSWERS

You need to understand when the answer is 'No'. You should be able to tell by the assistant's facial expression, tone of voice and gesture; but there are some language clues, such as:

No (it's not)	**Bù/ bùshì**
	Boo/Boo-shih
	不／不是
No there isn't	**Méiyǒu**
	May-yow
	没有
I don't have a railway timetable	**Méiyǒu huǒchē shíkèbiǎo**
	May-yow hwo-chuh shi-ko-byaow
	没有火车时刻表
None left	**Méiyǒu le**
	May-yow la
	没有了
It's free	**Miǎnfèi**
	Myenn-fay
	免费

Accommodations

Hotel

ESSENTIAL INFORMATION

If you want hotel-type accommodation, all the following words are
worth looking for on name boards

BĪNGUĂN	宾馆
FÀNDIÀN	饭店
DÀSHÀ	大厦
LǙGUĂN	旅馆
LǙDIÀN	旅店
ZHĀODÀISUŎ (Guest house)	招待所

Remember that:
- A booking through CITS will ensure that you have a room
  even in busy periods.
- Chinese hotels charge a bewildering variety of prices for
  different categories of room. Budget travellers are advised to
  show student cards and to be patient and persistent with
  Chinese staff who may encourage them to book more expensive rooms rather than cheap dormitory accommodation. The
  latter is usually available somewhere in the town: wait pa-
  tiently and say you are sure a room will become available soon.
- Hotels in large towns may offer Western as well as Chinese
  food, but in smaller places Chinese only is on offer.
- Chinese breakfast can consist of rice gruel and various cakes
  and buns. Western breakfast will usually involve some kind of
  eggs, bread, jam and coffee. Western-managed hotels offer
  internationally recognizable coffee shop fare.
- You will be asked to fill in a registration form (if travelling
  alone: otherwise your group guide will deal with it).
- Tipping has been frowned on in the People's Republic: it is
  normal practice in Hong Kong, Taiwan and Singapore.

[*Finding a hotel, see p.32*]

WHAT TO SAY

I have a booking	**Wǒ dìng fángzi le** Waw ding fang-dzi la 我订房子了

Have you any vacancies, please?	**Yǒu kōng fángzǐ ma?** Yow koong fang-dzi ma 有空房子吗?
Can I book a room?	**Kěyǐ dìng fángzǐ ma?** Ko-ee ding fang-dzi ma 可以订房子吗?
It's for one person	**Yīgè rénde** Ee-ga rin-da 一个人的
two people	**Liǎnggè rénde** Lyang-ga ren-de 两个人的

[For numbers, see p.128]

It's for ...	**Yào zhù ...** Yaow jew ... 要住
one night	**yī yè** ee-yeh 一夜
two nights	**liǎng yè** lyang yeh 两夜
one week	**yīgè xīngqī** ee-ga seeng-chee 一个星期
two weeks	**liǎnggè xīngqī** lyang-ga seeng-chee 两个星期
I would like ...	**Wǒ xiǎngyào ...** Waw syang-yaow ... 我想要
one/two	**yīgè/liǎnggè** ee-ga/lyang-ga 一个／两个
room(s) with a single bed	**dānchuáng fáng** dan-chwang fang 单床房
with two single beds	**shuāngchuáng fáng** shwang-chwang fang 双床房
with a double bed	**shuāngrén chuáng fáng** shwang-rin chwang fang 双人床房

with a toilet	**dài cèsuǒ**
	dai tsuh-swo
	带厕所
with a bathroom	**dài xǐzǎojiān**
	digh see-dzaow jyenn
	带洗澡间
with a shower	**dài línyù**
	digh lin-yoo
	带淋浴
with a cot	**dài értóng chuáng**
	digh urr-toong chwang
	带儿童床
with a balcony	**dài yángtái**
	digh yang-tigh
	带阳台
I would like ...	**Wǒ xiǎngyào ...**
	Waw syang-yaow ...
	我想要...
full board	**quán bāo huǒshí**
	chwann baow hwo-shir
	全包伙食
half board	**bàn bāo huǒshí**
	bann baow hwo-shir
	半包伙食
bed and breakfast	**chuángwèi hé zǎofàn**
	chwang-way ho dzow-fann
	床位和早饭
Do you serve meals?	**Nǐmen zhèr guǎnfàn ma?**
	Nee-min jurr gwann-fann ma
	你们这儿管饭吗?
At what time is ...	**Jǐdiǎn ...**
	Jee-dyenn ...
	几点
breakfast?	**chī zǎofàn?**
	chir dzaow-fann
	吃早饭?
lunch?	**chī wǔfàn?**
	chir woo-fan
	吃午饭?
dinner?	**chī wǎnfàn?**
	chir wan-fan
	吃晚饭?
How much is it?	**Duōshǎo qián?**
	Daw-shaow chyenn
	多少钱?

Can I look at the room?	**Kěyǐ kàn fángzi ma?** Ko-ee kan fang-dzi ma 可以看房子吗?
I'd prefer a room ...	**Wǒ xiǎng yaò ...** Waw syang-yaow ... 我想要...
at the front/ at the back	**qiánbiānde fángzi/hòubiānde fángzi** chyenn-byenn-di fang-dz/how-byenn-di fang-dz 前边的房子/后边的房子
OK, I'll take it	**Hǎo, zū zhèi fángzi** Haow, dzoo jay fang-dzi 好, 租这房子
No thanks, I won't take it	**Xièxie, bù yàole** Sie-sie, boo yaow-la 谢谢, 不要了
The key to number (ten), please	**(Shí) hào de yàoshí** (Shir) haow di yaow-shir (十)号的钥匙
Please may I have ...	**Qǐng gěi wǒ ...** Cheeng gay waw ... 请给我...
a coat hanger	**yīfú jià** yee-foo jya 衣服架
a towel	**máojīn** maow-jeen 毛巾
a glass	**bēizi** bay-dz 被子
some soap	**féizào** fay-dzaow 肥皂
an ashtray	**yānhuīgǎng** yenn-hway-gang 烟灰缸
another pillow	**lìng yígè zhěntóu** leeng ee-ga jinn-tow 另一个枕头
another blanket	**lìng yígè tǎnzi** leeng ee-ga tan-dz 另一个毯子

Come in!	**Qǐng jìn!** Cheeng jeen! 请进!
One moment, please!	**Děngyīděng** Dung-ee-dung 等一等
Please can you ...	**Qǐng nǐ ...** Cheeng nee ... 请你...
do this laundry/dry cleaning?	**bǎ zhè sòng xǐyǐdiàn/gānxǐ?** ba jay soong see-yee-dyenn/gan-see 把这送洗衣店／干洗?
call me at (seven o'clock)?	**(qī diǎn) dǎ diànhuà?** (chee dyenn) da dyenn-hwa (七点) 打电话?
help me with my luggage?	**bāng wǒ bān xínglǐ?** bang-waw ban seeng-lee 帮我搬行李?
call me a taxi for ...? *(for times see p.133)*	**... diǎn jiào chē?** ... dyenn jow chuh ...点叫车?
The bill, please	**Qǐng suànzhàng** Cheeng swann-jang 请算帐
Is service included?	**Bāokuò fúwùfèi ma?** Bow-kwo foo-woo-fay ma 包括服务费吗?
I think this is wrong	**Hǎoxiàng bú duì** How-syang boo-dway 好像不对
Can you give me a receipt?	**Néng gěi wǒ shōujù ma?** Nung gay waw show-joo ma 能给我收据吗?

At breakfast

Some more ... please	**Qǐng duō lái ...** Qing daw ligh ... 请多来...
coffee	**kāfēi** ka-fay 咖啡

tea	**chá** char 茶
bread	**miànbāo** myenn-bow 面包
butter	**huángyóu** hwang-yow 黄油
iam	**guǒjiàng** gwo-jyang 果酱
May I have a boiled egg?	**Qǐng lái zhǔ jīdàn?** Cheeng ligh jew jee-dan 请来煮鸡蛋

LIKELY REACTIONS

Have you a passport/ travel permit?	**Hùzhào? / Lǚxíngzhèng?** Hoo-jaow / Loo-sing-jung 护照/旅行证?
What's your name? [see p.19]	**Nín guìxìng?** Neen gway-seeng 您贵姓?
Sorry, we're full.	**Fángzi dōu mǎnle** Fang-dz dow man-la 房子都满了
I haven't any rooms left	**Méiyǒu fángzi** May-yow fang-dz 没有房子
Do you want to have a look?	**Yào kànkàn ma?** Yaow kan-kan ma 要看看吗?
How many people is it for?	**Zhù jǐge rén?** Jew jee-ga rin 住几个人?
From 7 o'clock onwards	**Cóng qīdiǎn kāishǐ** Tsoong chee-dyenn kigh-shir 从七点开始
From mid-day onwards	**Cóng zhōngwǔ kāishǐ** Tsoong joong-woo kigh-shir 从中午开始
[For times, see p.133]	
It's 60 dollars	**Liùshí kuài qián** Lyoo-shir kwai chyenn 六十块钱
[For numbers, see p.128]	

Rented accommodations: problem solving

ESSENTIAL INFORMATION

- If you are renting accommodation, you will need to know:
ZŪ FÁNGZI (rent a house or flat)	租房子
LÓU FÁNG (flats)	楼房
SÌ HÉ YUÀN (courtyard house)	四合院
HUĀYUÁN (garden)	花园
FÁNGZŪ (the rent)	房租
- For arranging the details of your let, see 'Hotel' p.32.
- Key words you will meet if renting on the spot:
BĂOZHÈNGJĪN (deposit)	保证金
YÀOSHI (key)	钥匙
- On arrival in your flat, check that the basic amenities are working. You may find limited cooking facilities with bottled gas, lamps with rather low wattage, insect repellent in summer (mosquito nets are common) and electricity supply which can be affected by power cuts, so be careful about the appliances you use. Air-conditioners are becoming more common; simple rush mats to shade the windows in summer are a cheaper alternative. Emergency contact: establish whom to contact in an emergency, even if it is only a neighbour in the first instance.
- Central heating is available north of the Yangtze only, so winters in cities like Xian and Shanghai can be very chilly.

WHAT TO SAY

My name is ...	**Wǒ xìng ...**
	Waw seeng ...
	我姓
I'm staying at ...	**Wǒ zhù ...**
	Waw jew ...
	我住
They've cut off ...	**Tāmen ba ... duàntíngle**
	Ta-min ba ... dwann-ting la
	他们把...断停了

the electricity	**diànyuán** dienn-ywann 电源
the gas	**méiqì** may-chee 煤气
the water	**shuǐ** shway 水
Is there ... in the area?	**Zhèr yǒu ... ma?** Jurr yow ... ma 这儿有…吗?
an electrician	**diàngōng** dyenn-goong 电工
a plumber	**guǎnzi gōng** gwann-dz goong 管子工
a workman	**xiūlǐ gōng** syoo-lee goong 修理工
Where is ...	**... zài nǎr?** ... dzigh narr …在哪儿?
the fuse box?	**Bǎoxiǎn sī** Bow-syenn si 保险丝
the stopcock?	**Guǎnshuān** Gwann-shwann 管闩
the boiler?	**Diànlú** Dyenn-loo 电炉
the hot water?	**Rè shuǐ** Ruh shway 热水
Is there ...	**Zhèr yǒu ...?** Jurr you ... 这儿有…?
town gas?	**guǎndào méiqì ma?** gwann-daow may-chee ma 管道煤气吗?
bottled gas?	**píngzhuāng méiqì ma?** ping-jwang may-chee ma 瓶装煤气吗?

mains drainage?	**xiàshuǐdào zǒngguǎn ma?** sya-shway-daow dzoong-gwan ma 下水道总管吗?
a septic tank?	**huàfèn chí ma?** hwa-fin chir ma 化粪池吗?
central heating?	**nuǎnqì ma?** nwann-chee ma 暖气吗?
The cooker	**Lúzi** Loo-dz 炉子
The hairdryer	**Diàn chuīfeng** Dyenn chway-fung 电吹凤
The heating	**Nuǎnqì** Nwan-chee 暖气
The immersion heater	**Diàn rèshuǐqì** Dyenn ruh-shway-chee 电热水器
The iron	**Yùndǒu** Yoon-dow 熨斗
The refrigerator	**Bīngxiāng** Beeng-syang 冰箱
The telephone	**Diànhuà** Dyenn-hwa 电话
The toilet	**Cèsuǒ** Tsuh-swo 厕所
The washing machine	**Xǐyījī** See-ee-jee 洗衣机
... is not working	**... huàile** ... hwai-la ... 坏了
Where can I get ...	**Nǎr néng zhǎo ...** Narr nung jow ... 哪儿能找...

an adaptor for this? **yòng zhèrde jìdiànqì?**
yoong-jerd jee-dyenn-chee
用这儿的继电器？

a bottle of gas? **yīpíng méiqì?**
yee-ping may-chee
一瓶煤气？

a fuse? **bǎoxiǎn sī?**
bow-syenn-si
保险丝？

an insecticide? **shāchóngjì?**
sha-choong-jee
杀虫剂？

a light bulb? **dēngpào**
dung-paow
灯泡？

The drain **Xiàshuǐdào ...**
Sya-shway-daow ...
下水道

The sink **Shuǐ chízi ...**
Shway chir-dz ...
水池子

The toilet **Cèsuǒ ...**
Tsuh-swo ...
厕所

... is blocked **dǔle**
doo-la
堵了

The gas is leaking **Lòu qì le**
Low chee-la
漏气了

Can you mend it straightaway? **Qǐng mǎshàng xiūlǐ**
Cheeng ma-shang syoo-lee
请马上修理

When can you mend it? **Shénme shíhou néng xiūlǐ?**
Shumma shi-how nung syoo-lee
什么时候能修理？

How much do I owe you? **Gāi fù duōshǎo qián?**
Guy foo daw-shaow chyenn
该付多少钱？

When is the rubbish collected? **Shénme shíhou shōu lājī?**
Shumma shi-how show la-jee
什么时候收垃圾？

LIKELY REACTIONS

What's your name?	**Nín guìxìng?** Neen gway-seeng 你贵姓?
What's your address?	**Nǐde dìzhǐ?** Nee-di dee-jih 你的地址?
There's a shop ...	**... yǒu shāngdiàn** ... yow shang-dyenn ...有商店
in town	**Chénglǐ** Chung-lee 城里
in the village	**Cūnzi lǐ** Tsoon-dz lee 村子里
I can't come ...	**... bù néng lái** ... boo nung ligh ...不能来
today	**Jīntiān** Jeen-tyenn 今天
this week	**Zhèi xīngqī** Jay seeng-chee 这星期
until Monday	**Xīngqīyī yǐqián** Seeng-chee-ee ee-chyenn 星期一以前
I can come on Tuesday	**Wǒ Xīngqīèr lái** Waw Seeng-chee-urr ligh 我星期二来
I can come when you want	**Nǐ yuē shíjiān wǒ jiù lái** Nee yweh shi-jenn waw jew ligh 你约时间我就来
Every day	**Měitiān** May-tyenn 每天
Every other day	**Měi liǎng tiān** May lyang tyenn 每两天
On Wednesdays [*For days of the week, see p.136*]	**Xīngqīsān** Seeng-chee-san 星期三

General shopping

The Pharmacy/The chemist's

ESSENTIAL INFORMATION

- Look for the words
  YÀO FÁNG (chemist, dispensary)　　　药房
  YÀODIÀN (chemist's)　　　　　　　　药店
  YĪYÀO SHĀNGDIÀN (chemist shop)　医药商店
- Medicines (drugs) are only available at a chemist's and you can choose between Chinese traditional medicine or Western drugs. Chinese friends, or your guide, will recommend a suitable Chinese medicine for your complaint.
- Chemists are competent to treat minor illnesses.
- Large hotels, airports and railway stations all have first-aid rooms and staff with some level of medical training on hand to deal with emergencies.
- Hotels, friendship shops and department stores also sell some non-drugs, like aspirin, or medicines for the common cold.
- Chinese medicines and acupuncture are very effective for some conditions, so if you are interested, do try them out.
- If you have an emergency, a large hospital may be the best place to try, or your hotel will arrange for a doctor to visit you.
- Unlike chemists in the West, the Chinese chemist shop has no cosmetics and toiletries section. To buy these, look for a department store (百货商店　bǎihuò shāngdiàn) or a general store (日用品商店　rìyòngpǐn shāngdiàn).
- Chemists are open during normal shopping hours, i.e. from 9 a.m. to 6.30 p.m. every day including Sunday, and a few chemists take it in turn to stay open all night.

[*Finding a chemist, see p.43*]

WHAT TO SAY

I'd like ...	**Wǒ xiǎngyào ...**
	Waw syang-yaow ...
	我想要…
some Alka-Seltzer	**jiǎnxìng kuàngquán shuǐ**
	jyenn-seeng kwang-chwann shway
	碱性矿泉水
some antiseptic	**xiāo dú shuǐ**
	syow doo shway
	消毒水

some aspirin	**āsīpǐlín** a-si-pee-lin 阿司匹林
a bandage	**bēngdài** bung-digh 绷带
some cotton wool	**tuōzhī mián** two-jr mienn 脱脂绵
some eye drops	**yǎnyào shuǐ** yenn-yaow shway 眼药水
some foot powder	**jiǎo qì fěn** jyaow-chee-fin 脚气粉
some gauze dressing	**shābù** sha-boo 纱布
some inhalant	**bèi xīrù de yàopǐn** bay see-roo de yaow-pin 被吸入的药品
some insect repellent	**fángchóng jì** fang-choong-jee 防虫剂
some lip salve	**chún gāo** choon gaow 唇膏
some nose drops	**dībí yào** dee-bee yaow 滴鼻药
sleeping tablets	**ānmián yào** an-myenn yaow 安眠药
some sticking plaster	**xiàngpí gāo** syang-pee gaow 橡皮膏
some throat pastilles	**késou piàn** ko-sow pyenn 咳嗽片
some Vaseline	**Wēishìlín** Way-shi-leen 威士林

I'd like something for ...	**Wǒ xiǎngyào zhì ... de yào**
	Waw syang-yaow jih ... de yaow
	我想要治...的药
bites	**chóng yǎo**
	choong yaow
	虫咬
burns	**shāo shāng**
	shaow shang
	烧伤
chilblains	**dòng chuáng**
	doong chwang
	冻疮
a cold	**gǎnmào**
	gann maow
	感冒
a cough	**késou**
	ko-sow
	咳嗽
diarrhoea	**là dùzi**
	la doo-z
	辣肚子
earache	**ěrduo téng**
	urr-do tung
	耳朵疼
flu	**liú gǎn**
	lyew gann
	流感
scalds	**tàng shāng**
	tang shang
	烫伤
sore gums	**yá chuáng téng**
	ya chwang tung
	牙床疼
sprains	**niǔ shāng**
	nyew shang
	扭伤
bee stings	**fēng zhē**
	fung juh
	蜂蛰
mosquito bites	**wénzi dīng**
	winn-dz deeng
	蚊子叮
sunburn	**zhuó shāng**
	jwaw shang
	灼伤

car (sea/air) sickness	**yùnchē** yoon-chuh 晕车
I need ...	**Wǒ xūyào ...** Waw soo-yaow ... 我需要...
some contraceptives	**bìyùn yào** bee-yoon yaow 避孕药
some deodorant	**fáng chòu jì** fang chow jee 防臭剂
some hand cream	**shǒugāo** show-gaow 手膏
some lipstick	**kǒuhóng** kow-hoong 口红
some make-up remover	**jiémiànshuǐ** jye-mienn-shway 洁面水
some paper tissues	**wèishēng zhǐ** way-shung jir 卫生纸
some razor blades	**guāhú dào** gwa-hoo daow 刮胡刀
some safety pins	**ānquán biézhēn** an-chwan bye-jun 安全别针
some sanitary towels	**yuèjīng dài** ywe-jeeng digh 月经带
some shampoo	**xǐtóushuǐ** see-tow-shway 洗头水
some shaving cream	**tì húzi yòngde gāo** tee hoo-dz yoong-di gaow 剃胡子用的膏
some soap	**féizào** fay-dzaow 肥皂
some sun-tan lotion/oil	**fáng shài gāo/yóu** fang shai gaow/yow 防晒膏／油

some talcum powder	**shuǎngshēn fěn** shwang-shin fin 爽身粉
some Tampax	**yuèjīng miánsāi** ywe-jeeng mienn sigh 月经棉塞
some toilet paper	**wèishēng zhǐ** way-shung jir 卫生纸
some toothpaste	**yágāo** ya-gaow 牙膏

FOR BABY

- Disposable nappies are hard to find in China. Some Friendship Stores sell them, at a high price.
- Baby foods and infant formula are sold where the sign 儿童食品 Értóng shípǐn is seen.
- Baby clothes are sold in the children's departments of big stores, 童装部 Tóngzhuāng bù.
- Cotton nappies, 尿布 Niàobù, are usually home-made. Ask a Chinese friend about getting hold of some.

CHINESE MEDICINES

Some Chinese remedies are well known and effective. Here are some of the most common ones.

gǎnmào chōngjì	cold medicine 感冒冲剂
bǎnlán' gēn chōngjì	flu medicine 板蓝根冲剂
niúhuáng jiědú piān	bezoar (for constipation) 牛黄解毒片
huángliánsù	coptis chinensis (for diarrhoea) 黄连素
báiyào	white powder (stops bleeding) 白药
qīngliángyóu	tiger balm (for headaches, fever) 清凉油
gān cǎo piān	licorice root pill (for coughs) 甘草片
liù shén wán	tiny pills for sore throats 六神丸

[For other essential expressions, see 'Shop talk', p.60]

Vacation items

ESSENTIAL INFORMATION

- Places to shop at and signs to look for:
  SHŪDIÀN (bookshop)   书店
  YĀNCĂODIÀN (tobacconist)   烟草片
  MĔISHÙ SHĀNGDIÀN (souvenirs, regional crafts)   美术商
  ZHÀOXIÀNGGUĂN (photographic supplies)   照相馆
  Department stores:
  YŎUYÌ SHĀNGDIÀN Friendship Store - restricted to non-
  Chinese nationals and their friends   友谊商
  BĂIHUÒ SHĀNGDIÀN/BĂIHUÒ DÀLÓU Department sto
       百货商
       百货人

WHAT TO SAY

Where can I buy ... ?	**Dào năr qù măi ... ?** Dow nar chew mye ... 到哪儿去买?
I'd like ...	**Wŏ xiăngyào ...** Waw syang-yaow ... 我想要...
a bag	**yīge kŏu dai** ee-ga kow-digh 一个口袋
a beach ball	**yīge zúqiú** ee-ga dzoo-chew 一个足球
a bucket	**yīge shuĭtŏng** ee-ga shway-toong 一个水桶
an English newspaper	**Yīngwén bàozhĭ** Eeng-win baow-jih 英文报纸
some envelopes	**xìnfēng** seen-fung 信封
a guide book	**zhĭnánshū** jih-nan-shoo 指南书
a map of the area	**dìtú** dee-too 地图

some postcards	**míngxìnpiàn** meeng-seen-pyenn 明信片
a spade	**chǎnzi** chan-dz 铲子
a straw hat	**cǎomào** tsao-maow 草帽
a suitcase	**shǒutíbao** show-tee-bow 手提包
some sun-glasses	**tàiyáng jìng** tigh-yang jing 太阳镜
a sunshade	**yángsǎn** yang-san 阳伞
an umbrella	**yǔsǎn** yew-san 雨伞
some writing paper	**xìnzhǐ** seen-jih 信纸
I'd like ... (*show the camera*)	**Wǒ xiǎngyào ...** Waw syang-yaow ... 我想要...
a colour film	**cǎisè jiāojuǎn** tsigh-suh jow-jwann 彩色胶卷
a black-and-white film	**hēibái jiāojuǎn** hay-bye jyow-jwann 黑白胶卷
for prints	**wèi túpiàn** way too-pyenn 为图片
for slides	**zuò huàndēng** dzaw hwann-dung 做幻灯
12/24/36 exposures	**shíèr/èrshísì/sānshíliù zhāng de** shi-urr/urr-shi-si/san-shi-lyoo jang ai 十二/二十四/三十六张的

a standard 8-mm film	**biāozhǔnde bā gōnglí jiāojuǎn**
	byow-joon-di ba-goonglee jyow-jwann
	标准的八公厘胶卷
a super-8 film	**tèjí bāpái jiāojuǎn**
	tuh-jee ba-pigh jyow-jwann
	特级八牌胶卷
some flash bulbs	**shǎnguāng dēng**
	shann-gwang dung
	闪光灯
This camera is broken	**Zhàoxiàngjí huàile**
	Jaow-syangjee-why-la
	照相机坏了
The film is stuck	**Jiāojuǎn bù zhuǎnle**
	Jyaow-jwann boo jwann-la
	胶卷不转了
Please can you ...	**Qǐng nǐ ...**
	Cheeng nee ...
	请你
develop/print this?	**chōngxǐ zhèige**
	choong-see jay-ga
	冲洗这个
load the camera?	**báng wǒ zhuāng jiāojuǎn?**
	bang waw jwang jyaow-jwann
	帮我装胶卷
Lighter fuel	**Dǎhuǒjī yòngde qìyóu**
	Da-hwo-jee yoong-di chee-yow
	打火机用的汽油
Lighter gas, please	**Dǎhuǒjī yòngde qì**
	Da-huo-jee yong-di chee
	打火机用的气

[*For other essential expressions, see 'Shop talk', p.60*]

The tobacco shop

ESSENTIAL INFORMATION

- A tobacconist is called a YĀNCǍO DIÀN   烟草店

  To ask if there is one nearby, see p.24.
- Chinese tobacco is cured differently from others you are used to. A few foreign brands are available in international hotels.

WHAT TO SAY

A packet of cigarettes ...	**Yī hé yān** Ee ho yenn 一盒烟
with filters	**dài zuǐde** digh dzway-di 带咀的
without filters	**bù dài zuǐdi** boo digh dzway-di 不带咀的
menthol	**bòhe yān** baw-ho yenn 薄荷烟
Those up there ...	**Nàrde ...** Narr-di 那儿的
on the right	**zài yòubian** dzigh yow-byenn 在右边
on the left	**zài zuǒbian** dzigh dzo-byenn 在左边
Those (*point*)	**Nèixie** Nay-sye 那些
Cigarettes please ...	**Mǎi yānjuǎn** Migh yen-jwan 买烟卷
100, 200, 300	**yībǎi, èrbǎi, sānbǎi** ee-bigh, urr-bigh, san-bigh 一百, 二百, 三百

Two packets	**Liǎng bāo** Lyang baow 两包
Do you have ...	**Yǒuméiyǒu ...** Yow-may-yow ... 有没有...
English cigarettes?	**Yīngguó yānjuǎn?** Eeng-gwo yenn-jwann 英国烟卷？
American cigarettes?	**Měiguó yānjuǎn?** May-gwo yenn-jwann 美国烟卷？
pipe tobacco?	**yāndǒu yòngde yān?** yenn-dow yoong-di yenn 烟斗用的烟？
rolling tobacco?	**yānsī?** yenn-si 烟丝？
A packet of pipe tobacco?	**Yīhé yāndǒu yòngde yān?** Ee-ho yenn-dow yoong-di yenn 一盒烟斗用的烟？
That one there ..	**Nèige** Nay-ga 那个
on the right	**zài yòu** dzigh-yow 在右
on the left	**zài zuǒ** dzigh dzo 在左
A cigar, please	**Qǐng gěi wǒ yīzhī xuějiā** Cheeng gay waw ee-jir swe-jya 请给我一枝雪茄
This one (*point*)	**Zhèige** Zhay-ga 这个
A box of matches	**Yī hé huǒchái** Ee-he hwo-chae 一盒火柴
A packet of flints (*show lighter*)	**Yīhé dǎhuǒ shí** Yee-ho da-hwo shir 一盒打火石

Buying clothes

ESSENTIAL INFORMATION

- Look for:
  NÜZHUĀNG (女装) (women's clothes)
  NÁNZHUĀNG (男装) (men's clothes)
  YÒUZHUĀNG (幼装) (children's clothes)
  PÍXIÉ/BÙXIÉ (皮鞋／布鞋) (leather/cloth shoes)
- Don't buy without being measured first or without trying things on.
- Don't rely on conversion charts of clothing sizes.
- If you are buying for someone else, take their measurements with you.

WHAT TO SAY

I'd like ...	**Qǐng gěi wǒ ...**
	Cheeng gay waw ...
	请给我...
an anorak	**dàimào de duǎnwàiyī**
	dye-mow di dwann-wigh yee
	带帽的短外衣
a belt	**yīge dàizi**
	ee-ga dye-dz
	一个带子
a bikini	**bǐ jī ní**
	bee-jee-nee
	比基尼
a bra	**yīfù nǎizhào**
	ee-foo nigh-jow
	一付奶罩
a swimming cap	**yóuyǒng màozi**
	yow-yoong mow-dz
	游泳帽了
a skiiing cap	**huáxué màozi**
	hwa-swe mow-dz
	滑雪帽子
a cardigan	**xíng shēn shì**
	seeng shen shir
	形身式

a coat	**cháng dàyì**
	chang da-ee
	长大衣
a dress	**nǚ xīfú**
	noo see-foo
	女西服
a hat	**màozi**
	mao-dzi
	帽子
a jacket	**jiākè**
	jia-ko
	茄克
a jumper	**máoyī**
	mao-ee
	毛衣
a night-dress	**shuìqún**
	shway-choon
	睡裙
a pair of pyjamas	**shuìyī**
	shway-ee
	睡衣
a pullover	**V-zi lǐng máoyī**
	Vay z leeng maow-ee
	V 字领毛衣
a raincoat	**yǔyī**
	yew-ee
	雨衣
a shirt	**chènshān**
	chen-shan
	衬衫
a skirt	**qúnzi**
	choon-dz
	裙子
a suit	**yī tào xīzhuāng**
	ee taow see-jwang
	一套西装
a swimsuit	**yóuyǒngyī**
	yow-yoong-ee
	游泳衣
a T-shirt	**T xuè**
	T swee
	T 恤
I'd like a pair of ...	**Xiǎng mǎi ...**
	Syang migh ...
	想买

shorts	**duǎnkù** dwann-koo 短裤
stockings	**chángtǒngwà** chang-toong-wa 长统袜
tights	**dàikù chángtǒng wà** dye-koo chang-toong-wa 带裤长统袜
briefs	**nǚ kùchǎ** noo ku-cha 女裤衩
gloves	**shǒutào** show-taow 手套
jeans	**lǎba kùzi** la-ba koo-dz 喇叭裤子
socks	**wàzi** wa-dz 袜子
trousers	**kùzi** koo-dz 裤
leather shoes	**píxié** pee-sye 皮鞋
cloth shoes	**bùxié** boo-sye 布鞋
sandals	**liángxié** lyang-sye 凉鞋
smart shoes	**piàoliangde xiézi** pyao-lyang di sye-dz 漂亮的鞋子
boots	**xuézi** swe-dz 靴子
moccasins	**biànxié** byenn-sye 便鞋
My size is ...	**Wǒ chuàn ... hào** Waw chwann ... haow
(*For numbers, see p.128*)	我穿...号

Can you measure me, please?	**Qǐng gěi wo liángba?** Cheeng gay waw lyang-ba 请给我量吧?
Can I try it on?	**Wǒ shìshi kàn, hǎoma?** Waw shi-shi kan, hao-ma 我试试看，好吗?
It's for a present	**Shì lǐwù** Shi lee-woo 是礼物
These are the measurements (*show written*)	**Yào zhèmme dà de** Yaow jumma da-di 要这么大的
chest/bust	**xiōng** syoong 胸
collar	**lǐng** ling 领
hips	**túnbù** toon-boo 臀部
leg	**tuǐ** tway 腿
waist	**yāo** yaow 腰
Have you got something ...	**Yǒuméiyǒu ...** Yow-may-yow 有没有...
in black?	**hēisède?** hay-suh-di 黑色的?
in white?	**báisède?** bigh-suh-di 白色的?
in grey?	**huīsède?** whey-suh-di 灰色的?
in blue?	**lánsède?** lan-suh-di 蓝色的?
in brown?	**huángsède?** hwang-suh-di 黄色的?

in pink?	**qiǎnhóng sède?** chyenn-hoong suh-di 浅红色的?
in green?	**lùsède?** loo-suh di 绿色的?
in red?	**hóngsède?** hoong-suh-di 红色的?
in yellow?	**huángsède?** hwang-suh di 黄色的?
in this colour? (*point*)	**zhèige yánsè de?** jay-ga yen-suh di 这个颜色的?
in cotton?	**miánbùde?** myenn-boo-di 棉布?
in silk?	**sīchóu de?** ssi-chow di 丝绸的?
in leather?	**pígéde?** pee-ga-di 皮革的?
in nylon?	**nílóngde?** nee-loong-di 尼龙的?
in suede?	**xiǎo shānyáng píde?** syao shan-yang pee-di 小山羊皮的?
in wool?	**yángmáode?** yang-maow-di 羊毛的?
in this material? (*point*)	**zhèizhòng bùde?** jay-joong boo-di 这种布的?

[*For other essential expressions, see 'Shop talk', p.60*]

Replacing equipment

ESSENTIAL INFORMATION

- Look for these signs:
  RÌYÒNG PǏN SHĀNGDIÀN 日用品商店
  ZÁHUÒ DIÀN 杂货店器 (hardware)
- In a supermarket, look for this display
  杂货日用 ZÁHUÒ RÌYÒNG
- To ask the way to the shop, see p.23.
- At a hotel or hostel, try their shop first.

WHAT TO SAY

Have you got ...	Nǐmen yǒuméiyǒu ...
	Nee-min yow-may-yow ...
	你们有没有...
an adaptor?	**jìdiànqì?**
(*show appliance*)	jee-dyenn-chee
	继电器？
a bottle of gas?	**yīpíng méiqì?**
	ee-ping may-chee
	一瓶煤气？
a corkscrew?	**kāisāizuān?**
	kigh-sigh-dzwan
	开塞钻？
any disinfectant?	**xiāodú shuǐ?**
	syaow-doo shway
	消毒水？
a drying-up cloth?	**yī kuài bù?**
	ee kwai boo
	一块布？
any forks?	**chāzi?**
	cha-dz
	叉子？
a fuse? (*show old one*)	**bǎoxiǎn sī?**
	baow-syenn ssi
	保险丝？
an insecticide?	**shāchóng jì?**
	shao-choong jee
	杀虫剂？
a paper kitchen roll?	**wèishēng zhǐ?**
	way-shung jih
	卫生纸？

any knives?	**dàozi?**
	daow-dz
	刀子?
a light bulb?	**dēng pào?**
	dung paow
	灯泡?
a plastic bucket?	**sùliào shuǐtǒng?**
	soo-lyaow shway-toong
	塑料水桶?
a scouring pad?	**cáliàng yòngde bù?**
	tsa-lyang yoongd boo
	擦亮用的布?
a spanner?	**bānshǒu?**
	ban-show
	扳手?
a sponge?	**hǎimián?**
	high-myenn
	海棉?
any string?	**shéng?**
	shung
	绳?
any tent pegs?	**zhàngpeng zhuāng?**
	jang-pung jwang
	帐篷桩?
a tin-opener?	**kāiguàn dào?**
	kye-gwan-daow
	开罐刀?
a torch?	**huǒjù?**
	hwo-jew
	火炬?
any torch batteries?	**huǒjù yòngde diànchí?**
	hwo-jew yoong-di dyenn-chir
	火炬用的电池?
a universal plug (for the sink)?	**xǐdícáo de sāizi?**
	seedee-tsaow di sigh-dz
	洗涤槽的塞子?
a washing line?	**xǐyī shéng?**
	see-yee shung
	洗衣绳?
any washing powder?	**xǐyīfěn?**
	see-yee-fin
	洗衣粉?
any washing-up liquid?	**xǐdí shuǐ?**
	see-dee shway
	洗涤水!

a washing-up brush?	**xǐdí shuāzi?**
	see-dee shawah-dz
	洗涤刷子?

[For other essential expressions, see 'Shop talk', p.60]

Shop talk

ESSENTIAL INFORMATION

- Know your coins and notes (see p.105).
- Know how to say the weights and measures.
- Be careful: the kilo is called the 'gongjin' or metric pound. The Chinese word 斤 *jīn* 'jeen' usually means a traditional Chinese pound equivalent to 500 grams. The words used here are those you find in shops. If you want to speak in grams, look up the numbers on page 128 and use the word 克 *kè*. E.g. 150 grams of biscuits would be 'yībǎi wǔshí kè bǐnggān' or more usually 'sān liǎng bǐnggān' – three *liǎng* of biscuits. You don't need a word for 'of': in Chinese, say one *jīn* meat, one litre milk, etc.
- The number two is either 二 èr or 两 liǎng before a quantity or amount of something. It can be confusing!

one 'liang' is 50 grams	**yī liǎng**
	ee lyang
	一两
100 grams	**èr liǎng**
	urr lyang
	二两
200 grams	**sì liǎng**
	sir lyang
	四两
½ kilo (one jin)	**yī jīn**
	ee jeen
	一斤
one kilo	**yī gōng jīn**
	ee goong jeen
	一公斤
two kilos	**liǎng gōng jīn**
	lyang goong jeen
	两公斤

½ litre	**bànshēng** ban-shung 半升
one litre	**yī shēng** ee shung 一升
two litres	**liǎng shēng** lyang-shung 两升

CUSTOMER

The self-service supermarket is a relative newcomer to China and is rarely found outside the major towns. It's often helpful to begin by catching the attendant's attention.

Hello	**Nǐ hǎo** Nee how 你好
Goodbye	**Zài jiàn** Dzigh jenn 再见
I'm just looking	**Wǒ zhǐ kànkàn** Wo jir kan-kan 我只看看
Excuse me	**Láo jià** or **Qǐng wèn** Lao ja or Cheeng win 劳驾 请问
How much is this/that?	**Zhège/nàge duōshǎo qián?** Jay-ga/na-ga daw-show chyenn 这个/那个多少钱?
What is that? (What are those?)	**Nà shì shénme?** Na shi shumma 那是什么?
Is there a discount?	**Kěyi piányì diǎn ma?** Kuh-ee pyenn-ee dyen ma 可以便宜点吗?

- NB: Bargaining is fine in the free market, but not in state-owned shops.

I'd like that please	**Wǒ yào nàge** Waw yaow na-ga 我要那个
Have you got something ...	**Nǐmen yǒu ...** Nee-men yow 你们有...

better?	**hǎo diǎnde ma?**
	how dyenn-di ma
	好点的吗?
cheaper?	**piányì diǎnde ma?**
	pyenn-ee dyenn-di ma
	便宜点的吗?
different?	**bù yíyàngde ma?**
	boo ee-yang-di ma
	不一样的吗?
larger?	**dà yīdiǎnde ma?**
	da ee-dyenn-di ma
	大一点的吗?
smaller?	**xiǎo yīdiǎnde ma?**
	syow ee-dyenn-di ma
	小一点的吗?
At what time ...	**Nǐmen shénme shíhou ...**
	Nee-min shumma shi-how ...
	你们什么时候...
do you open?	**kāi mén?**
	kigh minn
	开门?
do you close?	**guān mén?**
	gwann minn
	关门?
Can I have a bag please?	**Néng gěi wǒ yīge dàizi ma?**
	Nung gay waw ee-ga digh-dz ma
	能给我一个袋子吗?
Can I have a receipt?	**Néng gěi wǒ yīge shōujù ma?**
	Nung gay waw ee-ga show-joo ma
	能给我一个收据吗?
Do you take ...	**Nǐmen shōu ... ma?**
	Nee-min show ... ma
	你们收...吗?
renminbi?	**rénmínbì**
	rinn-meen-bee
	人民币
FEC?	**wàihuìquàn**
	wigh-whey-chwann
	外汇券
dollars/pounds?	**Měiyuán/Yīngbàng**
	May-ywann/Eeng-bang
	美元/英镑

| travellers' cheques? | **lǚyóu zhīpiào**
loo-yoe jir-pyow
旅游支票 |
| credit cards? | **xìnyòng kǎ**
seen-yoong ka
信用卡 |

SHOP ASSISTANT

Can I help you?	**Nǐ yào shénme?** Nee yaow shumma 你要什么?
What would you like?	**Nǐ xiǎng mǎi shénme?** Nee syang migh shumma 你想买什么?
Will that be all?	**Hái yào shénme?** High yaow shumma 还要什么?
Is that all?	**Hái yào biéde ma?** High yaow bye-di ma 还要别的吗?
Anything else?	**Hái yǒu ma?** High yoe ma 还有吗?
Would you like it wrapped?	**Yào bāoqǐlái ma?** Yow baow-chee-ligh ma 要包起来吗?
Sorry, none left	**Mǎi wánle** Migh wann-la 卖完了
I haven't got any	**Méi yǒule** May yoe-la 没有了
I haven't got any more	**Méi yǒu gèng duōde le** May yow gung daw-de-la 没有更多的了
How many do you want?	**Yào jǐge?** Yaow jee-ga 要几个?
How much do you want?	**Yào duōshǎo?** Yaow daw-shaow 要多少?
Is that enough?	**Gòu bù gòu?** Goe boo goe 够不够?

Shopping for food

Bread

ESSENTIAL INFORMATION

- The baker's shop is not a feature of China's food shopping.
  Only in overseas Chinese communities (Hong Kong, Taiwan,
  Singapore and Chinatowns in Europe and America) can baker's shops with Chinese customers be found. Most Chinese
  people eat rice or noodles as their staple, and bread is a snack
  food, usually taken on trips or picnics, and usually fairly sweet.
  Shops selling to foreigners in China's main cities usually have
  bread, including a rather good dense brown bread.
- To buy bread look out for:

FÙSHÍ SHĀNGDIÀN	General food store	副食品商店
TÁNGGUǑ ⎤ GĀODIǍN SHĀNGDIÀN ⎦	Sweet shop, cake shop	糖果糕点商店
GĀODIǍN BÙ	Cake department (of a general food store)	糕点部
MIÀNBĀO	Bread	面包

WHAT TO SAY

Some bread, please	**Qǐng gěi wǒ nà miànbāo** Cheeng gay waw na myenn-baow 请给我拿面包
A large loaf	**Dà gèrde** Da gur-da 大个儿的
A small loaf	**Xiǎo gèrde** Syaow gur-da 小个儿的
A bread roll	**Miànbāo juǎn** Myenn-baow jwann 面包卷
Sliced bread	**Miànbāo piàn** Myenn-baow pyenn 面包片

White bread	**Bái miànbāo**
	Bigh myenn-baow
	白面包
Brown bread	**Hēi miànbāo**
	Hay myenn-baow
	黑面包
Two loaves	**Liǎng kuài miànbāo**
	Lyang kwigh myenn-baow
	两块面包
Four bread rolls	**Sìge miànbāo juǎn**
	Si-ga myenn-baow jwann
	四个面包卷

[*For other essential expressions, see 'Shop talk', p.60*]

Cakes

ESSENTIAL INFORMATION

- Key words to look out for:

GĀODIĂN ⎤	Cake shop	糕点商店
SHĀNGDIÀN ⎦		
GĀODIĂN BÙ	Cake department	糕点部
GĀODIĂN	Cake(s)	糕点
DIĂNXĪN	Cake(s) or savoury snack(s).	点心

- There are very few Western style 'patisserie', cake and coffee shops in China. They are found only in the major cities. Most cake shops sell only Chinese style (Zhōngshì 中式) cakes.

WHAT TO SAY

The type of cake varies from region to region, and from season to season. If you want to buy cakes or biscuits by weight, point to your choice.

100 grams of ...	**Èrliǎng ...**
	Urr-lyang ...
	二两
200 grams of ...	**Sìliǎng ...**
	Si-lyang ...
	四两

half a kilo of ...

Bàn gōngjīn ...
Ban goong-jeen ...
半公斤

biscuits

bǐnggān
bing-gan
饼干

sponge cake

huángdàn gāo
hwang-dan gaow
黄蛋糕

A selection, please

Jǐ zhòng zài yīqí
Jee joong dzigh ee-chee
几种在一起

You may like to try some cakes, familiar and unfamiliar:

A cake like that please

Qǐng gěi wǒ nèiyàngde
Cheeng gay waw nay-yang-di
请给我那样的

An apple pie

Píngguǒ pái
Ping-gwo pigh
苹果排

A beanpaste cake

Lǜdòu gāo
Loo-dow gaow
绿豆糕

Seed cake

Táosù
Taow-soo
桃酥

Moon cake (eaten at mid-
autumn festival: many
different kinds)

Yuè bǐng
Yweh beeng
月饼

Sticky rice cake

Jiāng mǐ tiáo
Jyang mee tyaow
江米条

Crispy cakes

Sūpí diǎnxīn
Soo-pee dyenn-seen
酥皮点心

Sweet/savoury

tiánde/xiánde
tyenn-di/syenn-di
甜的/咸的

Date and rice cake (eaten during
Dragon Boat Festival)

Zòngzi
Dzoong-dzi
粽子

[*For other essential expressions, see 'Shop talk', p.60*]

Ice cream and sweets

ESSENTIAL INFORMATION

- Key words to look for:

BÍNG QÍ LÍN	Ice-cream	冰淇淋（冰激凌）
XŬE GĀO	Ice lolly	雪糕
TÁNG GUŎ DIÀN	Sweet shop	糖果店
LĚNG YĬN DIÀN	Cold drinks	冷饮店
GĀO DIĂN SHĀNG DIÀN	Cake shop	糕点商店

- There are not many varieties of ice-cream on sale. One well-known kind is:
  BĚI BĪNG YÁNG   北冰洋
- Ice-cream and ice lollies are sold mainly in summer.
- Sweets are on sale in many local shops and department stores. The different regions of China naturally produce their local favourite sweets. Some are sold in cake shops; others are sold at particular times of the year by street vendors. See 'tang hulu' below.

WHAT TO SAY

A ... ice, please	**Wǒ yào yīge ... bíngqílín** Waw yaow ee-ga ... beeng-jee-lin 我要一个...冰淇淋
strawberry	**cǎoméi** tsaow-may 草莓
chocolate	**qiǎokèlì** chyaow-ko-lee 巧克力
vanilla	**nǎiyóu** nigh-yow 奶油
A 50-cent one	**wǔ máo de** woo-maow-di 五毛的
A block of ice-cream	**Yī kuài bīngzhuān** Ee kwigh bing-jwan 一块冰砖
An ice lolly	**Yī zhī bīnggùn** Ee jih bing-goon 一支冰棍

A milk lolly	**Yī zhī nǎiyóu bīnggùn** Ee jih nigh-yow bing-goon 一支奶油冰棍
A chocolate wafer	**Wēifū qiǎokēlì** Way-foo chyaow-ko-lee 威夫巧克力
A packet of ...	**Yībāo ...** Ee-baow ... 一包 ...
100 grams of ...	**èrliǎng ...** urr-lyang ... 二两 ...
200 grams of ...	**sìliǎng ...** si-lyang 四两
chewing gum	**kǒuxiāng táng** kow-syang tang 口香糖
chocolates	**qiǎokēlì táng** chyaow-ko-lee tang 巧克力
mints	**bòhe táng** baw-ho tang 薄荷糖
sweets	**táng** tang 糖
toffees	**nǎitáng** nigh-tang 奶糖
haws in caramel (*sold in Peking in winter*)	**tánghúlu** tang-hoo-loo 糖葫芦

[*For other essential expressions see 'Shop Talk', p.60*]

At the supermarket

ESSENTIAL INFORMATION

- There are hardly any supermarkets in China. They are found only in the main cities.
  CHĀOJÍ SHÌCHĂNG 超级市场 (supermarket)
  ZÌXUĂN SHĀNGCIIĂNG 自选商场 (self-service)
- Key instructions on signs in the shop:
  RÙKŎU ENTRANCE 入口
  CHŪKŎU EXIT 出口
  SHŌUKUĂN TÁI CHECKOUT/TILL 收款台
  LÁNZI BASKETS 篮子
- Opening times are usually from 9 a.m. to 7 p.m. In a few big cities you will find some privately run supermarkets which stay open until 8 p.m. or so.
- Chinese people buy their rice, noodles and flour at government-run grain shops. These staple foods, and others like oil (varying from province to province) are rationed, and you may have to ask about buying some foods 'off ration'. If you are resident in China (not touring) there will be arrangements for your grain ration tickets (Liángpiào 粮票).
- Dairy products are not part of the normal Chinese diet. It is difficult to buy milk, butter and cheese outside the large cities with foreign residents. Big hotels will have milk and butter for western-style breakfast.
  Yoghurt can be found fairly easily.

WHAT TO SAY

Excuse me, please	**Qǐng wèn** Cheeng win 请问
Where can I find ... ?	**... zài nǎr?** ... dzigh nar ...在哪儿?
the biscuits	**Bǐnggān** bing-gan 饼干
the bread	**Miànbāo** Myenn-baow 面包

the butter	**Huángyóu** Hwang-yow 黄油
the cheese	**Rǔlào** Roo-laow 乳酪 myenn-tyaow 面条

[fresh pasta, called qiēmiàn (chye-myenn 切面) is sold at the
grain store, liángdiàn 粮店]

the rice	**Dàmǐ** da-mee 大米
the salt	**Yán** yenn 盐
the soy sauce	**Jiàngyóu** jyang-yow 酱油
the sugar	**Táng** tang 糖
the sweets	**Tángguǒ** tang-gwo 糖果
the tea	**Chá** **cha** 茶
the tinned vegetables	**Shūcài guàntóu** shoo-tsigh gwan-tow 疏菜罐头
the tinned foods	**Guàntóu** gwan-tow 罐头
the chocolate	**Qiǎokèlì** Chyaow-ko-lee 巧克力
the coffee	**Kāfēi** Ka-fay 咖啡
the cooking oil	**Shíyóu** Shih-yow 食油

peanut oil	**Huāshēng yóu** hwa-shung yow 花生油
corn oil	**Yùmǐ yóu** yoo-mee yow 玉米油
rape-seed oil	**Càizǐ yóu** tsigh-dz yow 菜子油
sesame oil	**Zhīma yóu** jih-ma yow 芝麻
the crisps	**Zhá tǔdòu** ja too-dow 炸土豆
the fresh fish (*sold whole, not cleaned*)	**Xiānyú** syenn-yoo 鲜鱼
the chicken/duck eggs	**Jīdàn/yādàn** jee-dan/ya-dan 鸡蛋/鸭蛋
the frozen foods	**Lěngdòng shípǐn** lung-doong shi-pin 冷冻饮品
the fruit	**Shuǐguǒ** shway-guo 水果
the fruit juice	**Guǒzhī** gwo-jih 果汁
the jam	**Guǒjiàng** gwo-jyang 果酱
the meat	**Ròu** row 肉
the milk	**Niúnǎi** nyoo-nigh 牛奶
the noodles	**Miàntiáo** myenn-tyaow 面条
the vegetables	**Shùcài** shoo-tsigh 疏菜

the vinegar	**Cù**
	tsoo
	醋
the wine	**Jiǔ**
	jew
	酒
the yoghurt	**Suān nǎi**
	swann-nigh
	酸奶

Fruit and vegetables

ESSENTIAL INFORMATION

- Key words to look out for:

SHŬIGUǑ	水果	(fruit)
SHŪCÀI	蔬菜	(vegetables)
CÀIDIÀN	菜店	(grocer)
ZÌYÓU SHÌCHǍNG	自由市场	(free market)

- Fruit and vegetable supplies in China are seasonal and regional. The southern parts of the country, with their mild climate, produce a good range of vegetables all year round (although local consumers often take second place to the export market) but in north China the winter diet is a monotonous round of cabbage and turnip.
- Take your own shopping bag. Packaging is very basic.
- Chinese cooking demands total freshness, and it's not unusual for people to buy vegetables daily. The free market offers a superior choice, at a premium.

WHAT TO SAY

250 grams of ...	**Wǔ liàng ...**
	Woo lyang ...
	五两
Half a kilo of ...	**Bàn gōng jīn ...**
	ban goong jeen ...
	半公斤
1 kilo of ...	**Yī gōng jīn ...**
	Ee goong jeen ...
	一公斤

1½ kilos of ...	**Sān jīn ...**
	san jeen ...
	三斤
2 kilos of ...	**Liǎng gōng jīn ...**
	Lyang goong jin ...
	两公斤
apples	**píngguǒ**
	ping-gwo
	苹果
bananas	**xiāngjiāo**
	syang-jyaow
	香蕉
cherries	**yīngtáo**
	eeng-taow
	樱桃
grapes	**pútáo**
	poo-taow
	葡萄
oranges	**júzǐ**
	joo-dz
	桔子
peaches	**táozǐ**
	tao-dz
	桃子
pears	**lí**
	lee
	梨
plums	**lǐzǐ**
	lee-dz
	李子
strawberries	**cǎoméi**
	tsao-may
	草莓
tangerines	**hóngjú**
	hoong-joo
	红桔
A pineapple, please	**Qǐng ná yīgè bōló**
	Cheeng na ee-ga bo-law
	请拿一个菠萝
A melon, please	**Qǐng ná yīgè tiánguā**
	Cheeng na ee-ga tyenn-gwa
	请拿一个甜瓜
A water melon, please	**Qǐng ná yīgè xīguā**
	Cheeng na ee-ga see-gwa
	请拿 个西瓜

½ a kilo of ...	**Bàn gōng jīn ...** ban goong jeen ... 半公斤
1 kilo of ...	**Yī gōng jīn ...** Ee goong jeen ... 一公斤
1½ kilos of ...	**Sān jīn ...** San jeen ... 三斤
2 kilos of ...	**Liǎng gōng jīn ...** Lyang goong jin ... 两公斤
aubergines	**qiézǐ** che-dz 茄子
beansprouts	**méngyá** mung-ya 萌芽
carrots	**hú luóbù** hoo lo-boo 胡萝卜
corn on the cob	**zhěng yùmì** jung yoo-mee 整玉米
green beans	**qīng dòu** cheeng dow 青豆
mushrooms	**mógū** maw-goo 蘑菇
onions	**yángcōng** yang-tsoong 洋葱
spring onions	**cōng** tsoong 葱
peppers	**qīngjiāo** cheeng-jyaow 青椒
potatoes	**tǔdòu** too-dow 土豆
pumpkins	**nánguā** nan-gwa 南瓜

spinach	**bōcài** baw-tsigh 菠菜
tomatoes	**fānqié** fan-chye 蕃茄
A bunch of ...	**Yī bǎ ...** Ee ba ... 一把
celery	**qíncài** cheen-tsigh 芹菜
parsley	**xiāngcài** syang-tsigh 香菜
A head of garlic	**Yī tòu suàn** Ee tow swann 一头蒜
A lettuce	**Wōjù** waw-joo 莴苣
A cauliflower	**Càihuā** Tsigh-hwa 菜花
A cabbage	**Yáng báicài** Yang bye-tsigh 洋白菜
A Chinese cabbage	**Dà báicài** Da bye-tsigh 大白菜
A cucumber	**Huángguā** Hwang-gwa 黄瓜
Like that, please	**Nà yàngde** Na yang di 那样的

These are some fruit and vegetables which may not be familiar.

làjiāo	辣椒	fresh chilli pepper
lìzhī	荔枝	lychee fruit
luóbù	萝卜	Chinese turnip
xuělí	雪梨	'Tientsin pears', sweet and crunchy

jiǔcài	韭菜	Chinese chives
ǒu	藕	lotus roots
sīguā	丝瓜	loofah gourd
shìzi	柿子	persimmon/sharon fruit
suànmiáo	蒜苗	garlic shoots
wōsǔn	莴笋	asparagus lettuce
yóucài	油菜	rape
zhúsǔn	竹笋	bamboo shoots

[*For other essential expressions, see 'Shop talk', p.60*]

Meat

ESSENTIAL INFORMATION

- Key words to look for:

RÒU	肉	(Meat)
RÒUDIÀN	肉店	(Butcher)
CÀI SHÌCHĂNG	菜市场	(Market)
FÙSHÍ SHĀNGDIÀN	副食商店	(Food Store)
JĪLÈI BU	鸡类部	(Poultry)
RÒUSHÍ BÙ	肉食部	(Meat department)
SHÚSHÍ BÙ	熟食部	(Cooked meats)

- Pork is sold separately from beef and lamb. The latter are usually on sale to China's Muslims or Húimín 回民 only.
- It is usually impossible to specify the cut of meat you want to buy. You simply ask for a certain weight. There is no price distinction between the various cuts of meat, except in a few places where you can ask for lean meat at a higher price.
- Uncooked offal is bought at the butcher's. Cooked meats, ham and sausages are sold at the cooked meats counter (Shúshíbù) 熟食部
- Poultry is sold separately.

WHAT TO SAY

For a joint, choose the type of meat, and then say how many people it is for.

Some beef please

Qǐng ná diǎn niúròu
Cheeng na dyenn nyoo-row
请拿点牛肉

Some lamb	**Qǐng ná diǎn yángròu** Cheeng na dyenn yang-row 请拿点羊肉
Some pork	**Qǐng ná diǎn zhūròu** Cheeng na dyenn jew-row 请拿点猪肉
Some veal	**Qǐng ná diǎn xiǎoniúròu** Cheeng na dyenn syaow-nyoo-row 请拿点小牛肉
Some steak	**Qǐng ná diǎn niúpái** Cheeng na dyenn nyoo-pigh 请拿点牛排
Some liver	**Qǐng ná diǎn gān** Cheeng na dyenn gan 请拿点肝
Some kidney	**Qǐng ná diǎn shèn** Cheeng na dyenn shin 请拿点肾
Some sausages	**Qǐng ná diǎn xiāngcháng** Cheeng na dyenn syang-chang 请拿点香肠
Some minced meat	**Qǐng ná ròuxiàn** Cheeng na row-syenn 请拿肉馅
Some pork chops	**Qǐng ná zhūpái** Cheeng na jew-pigh 请拿猪排
Some lamb chops	**Qǐng ná yángpái** Cheeng na yang-pigh 请拿羊排
A chicken	**yī zhǐ jī** ee jih jee 一只鸡
A tongue	**shétóu** shuh-tow 舌头

Other essential expressions [*see also 'Shop talk' p.60*]

Please can you mince it	**Qǐng jiǎo chéng xiàn** Cheeng jyaow chung syenn 请绞成馅

Please can you dice it?	**Qǐng qiē chěng xiǎokuài** Cheeng chyeh chung syaow- kwigh 请切成小块
Please can you trim the fat?	**Qǐng qiēqù féide** Cheeng chyeh-choo fay-da 请切去肥的
Please can you slice it?	**Qǐng qiē chéng piàn** Cheeng chyeh chung pyenn 请切成片

Fish

ESSENTIAL INFORMATION

- The place to look for:
  XIĀNYÚ DIÀN   鲜鱼部   (Fishmonger)
  SHŬICHĂNBÙ   水产部   (Fishmonger)
  YÚBÙ   鱼部   (Fish section)
- Availability of fish varies a great deal. Coastal areas are well served. In the interior, freshwater fish is often plentiful, but it can be difficult to find good quality fish outside the main markets. The free markets will sometimes have better fish at a higher price than the state-run market.
- Many varieties of fish familiar to us are not found in Chinese waters. Here we have listed the varieties you are likely to see, particularly when eating out.
- Fish is sold whole, and not cleaned. Large fish is sold by the slice. Shellfish is sold by weight.

WHAT TO SAY

Half a kilo of ...	**Bàn gōng jīn ...** ban goong jeen ... 半公斤
shrimps	**xiǎoxiā** syaow-sya 小虾
prawns	**dàxiā** da-sya 大虾

mussels	**bèilèi** bay-lay 贝类
Please give me some ...	**Qǐng gěi wǒ ...** Cheeng gay waw ... 请给我...
carp	**lǐyú** lee-yoo 鲤鱼
sardines	**shā dīng yú** sha ding yoo 沙丁鱼
squid	**mòyú** mo-yoo 墨鱼
eel	**shànyú** shan-yoo 鳝鱼
yellow fish	**huángyú** hwang-yoo 黄鱼
silver carp	**liányú** lyenn-yoo 鲢鱼
cuttle fish	**yóuyú** yow-yu 鱿鱼
crab	**pángxiè** pang-sye 螃蟹

Other essential expressions [see also 'Shop talk' p.60]

Please can you take the head off	**Qǐng qùdiào tóu** Cheeng choo-dyaow tow 请去掉头
Please can you clean them	**Qǐng qùdiào nèizàng** Cheeng choo-dyaow nay-dzang 请去掉内脏
Please can you fillet them	**Qǐng qièchéng piàn** Cheeng chye-chung pyenn 请切成片
I want a whole fish	**Wǒ xiǎngyào zhěnggè yú** Waw syang-yaow jung-ga yoo 我想要整个鱼

Eating and drinking out

Ordering a drink

ESSENTIAL INFORMATION

- The places to ask for [see p.23]
  CHÁ YUÁN/ ⎤ (tea house)   茶园，茶馆
  CHÁ GUĂN ⎦
  LĚNG YĬN DIÀN (café)   冷饮店
  KĀ FĒI TĪNG   (coffee shop) 咖啡厅
  JIŬ BĀ   (bar)   酒吧
- The most common is the café, serving soft drinks (usually very sweet), yoghurt, ice-cream, ice lollies, bread and cakes. Some have a sit-down area, some do not.
- Coffee shops are all for sitting down. They are generally of a higher standard of decoration than cafés, and serve coffee, milk (usually with added sugar), beer, soft drinks and cakes.
- There are not many bars. Most are found near or in major hotels. They serve beer and wine and Chinese spirits which are extremely strong. They often also serve snacks and hors d'œuvres since Chinese people do not generally drink alcohol without eating.

WHAT TO SAY

I'll have ... please	**Qǐng ná ...**
	Cheeng na ...
	请拿...
a black coffee	**yī bēi kāfēi**
	ee bay ca-fay
	一杯咖啡
a white coffee	**yī bēi kāfēi, jiā niúnǎi**
	ee bay ca-fay jya nyoo-nigh
	一杯咖啡，加牛奶
a tea with milk	**yībēi hóngchá, jiā niúnǎi**
	ee-bay hoong-cha, jya nyoo-nigh
	一杯红茶，加牛奶
a tea with lemon	**yī bēi níngméng chá**
	ee bay neeng-mung cha
	一杯柠檬茶

a green tea	**yī bēi lǜchá**
	ee bay lu- cha
	一杯绿茶
a glass of milk	**yī béi niúnǎi**
	ee bay nyoo-nigh
	一杯牛奶
two glasses of milk	**liǎng bēi niúnǎi**
	lyang bay nyoo-nigh
	两杯牛奶
a hot chocolate	**yī bēi rè qiǎokēlì**
	ee bay ruh chyaow-ko-lee
	一杯热巧克力
a mineral water	**yī bēi kuàngquánshuǐ**
	ee bay kwang-chwan-shway
	一杯矿泉水
a lemonade	**yī bēi qìshuǐ**
	ee bay chee-shway
	一杯汽水
an orangeade	**yī bēi júzǐshuǐ**
	ee bay joo-dz shway
	一杯橘子水
a fresh orange juice	**yī bēi xiān júzhī**
	ee bay syenn joo-jih
	一杯鲜橘汁
a beer	**yī bēi píjiǔ**
	ee bay pee-jew
	一杯啤酒
a draught beer	**yī bēi sǎnzhuāng píjiǔ**
	ee bay san-jwann pee-jew
	一杯散装啤酒
a black beer	**yī bēi hēi píjiǔ**
	ee bay hay pee-jew
	一杯黑啤酒
A glass of ...	**Yī bēi ...**
	Ee bay ...
	一杯...
Two glasses of ...	**Liǎng bēi ...**
	Lyang bay ...
	两杯...
red wine	**hóng pútáo jiǔ**
	hoong poo-taow jew
	红葡萄酒
white wine	**bái pútáo jiǔ**
	bigh poo-taow jew
	白葡萄酒

dry	**gān** gan 干
sweet	**tián** tyenn 甜
A bottle of ...	**Yī píng ...** Ee ping ... 一瓶...
sparkling wine	**yǒupào pútáojiǔ** yow-paow poo-taow-jew 有泡葡萄酒
champagne	**xiāngbīn** syang-been 香槟
A whisky ...	**Wēishì jì** Way-shi-jee 威士忌
with ice	**jiā bīng** jya bing 加冰
with water	**jiā shuǐ** jya shway 加水
with soda	**jiā sūdǎ** jya soo-da 加苏打
A gin and tonic	**Kuíníng dù sōngzǐ jiǔ** Kway-ning doo soong-dz jew 奎宁杜松子酒
A gin and bitter lemon	**Níngméng dù sōngzǐ jiǔ** Ning-mung doo soong-dz jew 柠檬杜松子酒
A brandy	**Báilándì** Bye-lan-dee 白兰地
A martini	**Mǎtíní** Ma-tee-nee 马提尼
A sherry	**Xībānyá pútáojiǔ** See-ban-ya poo-taow-jew 西班牙葡萄酒

If you want to try some Chinese spirits, look out for:

Máotái	茅台	fiery, aromatic, from Guizhou
Fēnjiǔ	汾酒	spirit, from Shanxi province
Dàqū, Tèqū	大曲，特曲	spirit, from Sichuan province
Wǔliángyè	五粮液	'five grain' liquor
Shàoxīngjiǔ	绍兴酒	rice wine, a little like sake

Other essential expressions:

Miss/waiter
Xiǎojiě/fúwúyuán
Syaow-jye/foo-woo-ywan
小姐／服务员

The bill, please
Qǐng jiézhàng
Cheeng jye-jang
请结帐

Where is the toilet, please?
Qǐng wèn, cèsuǒ zài nǎr?
Cheeng-win, tse-swo dzigh narr
请问，厕所在那儿？

Ordering a snack

ESSENTIAL INFORMATION

- For all the stories in the Western press about hamburgers and fried chicken being all the rage in China, there are really very few Western-style fast-food places in China. Those there are will be in big cities like Peking, Canton and Shanghai.
- Most Chinese people think of 'snack food' as an extra, not an alternative, to meals. There are wide local variations in the types of snack found: different kinds of rice and wheat-based dumplings, buns, noodles and gruel are appreciated by the locals of the various regions. In some parts of the country, everything is dipped in vinegar or a soy-sauce and vinegar mixture. In other places, chilli paste or sauce is a must with any kind of snack.
- For people staying in western-managed hotels, a list of normal snack food is given here, but don't forget to try Chinese breakfast, for a chance to sample the local variety.
- The places to look for:
  FĒNGWÈI XIǍOCHĪ   风味小吃   (Local snacks)
  XIǍOCHĪ DIÀN   小吃店   (Snack bar)

WHAT TO SAY

I'll have ... please	**Qǐng ná ...**
	Cheeng na ...
	请拿...
a cheese sandwich	**nǎilào sānmíngzhì**
	nigh-laow san-ming-jih
	奶酪三明治
a ham sandwich	**huǒtuǐ sānmíngzhì**
	hwo-tway san-ming-jih
	火腿三明治
a mushroom omelette	**mógū jīdànbǐng**
	mo-goo jee-dan-bing
	蘑菇鸡蛋饼
a ham omelette	**huǒtuǐ jīdànbǐng**
	hwo-tway jee-dan-bing
	火腿鸡蛋饼

You may wish to add to your order:

chips	**zhá tǔdòu**
	ja too-dow
	炸土豆
bread	**miànbāo**
	myenn-baow
	面包
toast	**kǎo miànbāo**
	kaow myenn-baow
	烤面包

Here are some Chinese snacks you may like to try:

wheaten cake	huǒshāo	火烧
fried dough twist	máhuā	麻花
new year cake	nián'gāo	年糕
savoury bun	bāozi	包子
savoury pancake	xiànbǐng	馅饼
soup dumplings	húndùn	馄饨
steamed dumplings	jiǎozi	饺子
fried dumplings	guōtiē	锅贴
rice dumplings in soup	tāng yuán	汤圆
fried roll	zhá miànquān	炸面圈
noodles	miàntiáo	面条
oil cake	yóubǐng	油饼
oil stick	yóutiáo	油条
date and rice parcel (wrapped in reed leaf)	zòngzǐ	棕子

At a restaurant

ESSENTIAL INFORMATION

- The place to ask for: fànguǎn 饭馆 [see p.23]
  You can eat at all these places:

FÀNGUǍN	饭馆	restaurant
FÀNDIÀN	饭店	hotel/restaurant
FÀNZHUĀNG	饭庄	(big) restaurant
CĀNGUǍN	餐馆	restaurant
CĀNTĪNG	餐厅	dining room/restaurant
CĀNCHĒ	餐车	restaurant car

- Few restaurants have menus displayed outside the entrance. If you are going with a large party, or if you want to be sure of a table, you should book in advance. Chinese restaurants in mainland China are very oversubscribed and you may have real difficulties in finding a seat, let alone a table, if you turn up on spec. You will be given a separate room and can discuss the menus and the price when booking. It's often wise to fix a price, specify a few dishes and let the restaurant choose for you. When you eat in the main part of a restaurant, you will either have a printed menu or a blackboard. Don't be surprised if certain dishes are unavailable. Food in China is still very seasonal, so look out for fresh vegetables in the market as a sign of what to ask for.
- Try to find out about local specialities. Each area produces its own dishes, like Peking duck, Sichuan's hot spicy tofu, Shanghai crab and so on.
- The order in which food is presented may surprise you. You might begin with a mixed hors d'œuvres plate, work through seafood, vegetables, duck and chicken, pork and beef, ending up with soup. Desserts are not usual, but restaurants used to foreigners may offer toffee apples or refreshing orange segments.
- Pork is the most common meat, except in Muslim areas, where mutton and beef predominate. Most Chinese people eat rather little meat. Vegetarians have a difficult time in China, however, since a little meat is added to almost everything, and it is difficult to convey to a Chinese waiter that you want no meat products of any kind used in preparing your meal.
- The kitchens in most restaurants are out of bounds, but if you are curious and politely persistent you may be able to persuade someone to show you round.

- Chinese people think of food as 'dishes' (meat, fish and vegetables - served communally in the centre of the table) and 'staple' (noodles, rice or other grain fillers). The more expensive the meal, the less likely that you will want to eat much rice or noodles. When ordering food, choose for the whole party, not person by person.
- China operates an early day. Lunch is usually served between 11.30 and 1 o'clock, supper between 5.30 and 8. Restaurants catering for foreigners usually keep later hours, but it is always best to check before setting out.
- Many restaurants in China use monosodium glutinate powder to make food look shiny and appetizing. If this 'taste powder' disagrees with you, ask them not to use it Bùyào fàng wèi jīng 不要放味精 .

How to use chopsticks

Place first chopstick between base of thumb and top of ring finger.

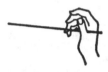

Hold second chopstick between top of the thumb and tops of middle and index fingers.

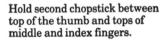

Keeping the first chopstick and thumb still, move the other one up and down by middle and index fingers.

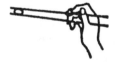

WHAT TO SAY

May I book a table?

Kěyǐ dìng zhuōzi ma?
Ko-yee deeng jwo-dz ma
可以订桌子吗?

I've booked ...

Wǒ dìngle ...
Waw ding-la ...
我订了...

a table for one	**yī rén yī zhuō** ee rin ee jwo 一人一桌
a table for three	**sān rén yī zhuō** san rin ee jwo 三人一桌
The menu, please	**Qǐng ná càidān** Cheeng na tsigh-dan 请拿菜单
What's this, please? (*point to the menu*)	**Qǐngwèn, zhèi shì shénme?** Cheeng-win jay shi shumma 请问，这是什么?
The wine list	**Jiǔ dàn** Jew dan 酒单
A bottle of beer, please	**Qǐng lái yī píng píjiǔ** Cheeng ligh ee ping pee-jew 请来一瓶啤酒
A glass of beer, please	**Qǐng lái yī bēi píjiǔ** Cheeng ligh ee bay pee-jew 请来一杯啤酒
Some soya sauce	**Yī diǎn jiàngyóu** Ee dyenn jyang-yow 一点酱油
Some vinegar	**Yī diǎn cù** Ee dyenn tsoo 一点醋
Some salt	**Yī diǎn yán** Ee dyenn yenn 一点盐
Some pepper	**Yī diǎn hǔjiāo** Ee dyenn hoo-jyaow 一点胡椒
How much does that come to?	**Yígòng duōshǎo qián?** Ee-goong dwo-shaow chyenn 一共多少钱?
Is service included?	**Bāokuò fùwú fèi ma?** Baow-kwo foo-woo fay ma 包括服务费吗?
Where is the toilet please?	**Qǐng wèn, cèsuǒ zài nǎr?** Cheeng win, tse-swo dzigh narr 请问，厕所在哪儿?
Miss!/Waiter!	**Xiǎojiě!/Fúwùyuán!** Syaow-jye!/Foo-woo-ywan 小姐!/服务员!

The bill, please	**Qǐng jiézhàng**
	Cheeng jye-jang
	请结帐
May I have a receipt?	**Qǐng gěi wǒ yīge shōujù**
	Cheeng gay waw ee-ga show-ju
	请给我一个收据

Key words for courses, as seen on some menus

[*Only ask this question if you want the waiter to remind you of the choice.*]

What have you got in the way of ...	**Nǐmen yǒu shénme ...**
	Nee-min yow shumma ...
	你们有什么...
STARTERS	**PĪNPÁN**
	peen-pan
	拼盘
SOUP	**TĀNG**
	Tang
	汤
EGG DISHES	**JĪDÀN**
	jee-dan
	鸡蛋
FISH	**XIĀNYÚ**
	syenn-yu
	鲜鱼
MEAT	**RÒU**
	row
	肉
GAME	**YĚ WEÌ**
	ye-way
	野味
FOWL	**JĪRÒU**
	jee-row
	鸡肉
VEGETABLES	**SHŪCÀI**
	shoo-tsigh
	蔬菜
CHEESE	**RǓLAÒ**
	roo-laow
	乳酪
FRUIT	**SHUǏGUǑ**
	shway-gwo
	水果

ICE-CREAM	BÍNGQÍLÍN
	beeng-jee-leen
	冰淇淋
DESSERT	DIǍNXĪN
	dyenn seen
	点心

UNDERSTANDING THE MENU

You will find the names of the principal ingredients of most dishes on these pages:

Meat, see p.76   Fruit, see p.73
Fish, see p.78   Dessert, see p.66
Vegetables, see p.74   Ice-cream, see p.67

Used together with the following lists of cooking and menu terms, they should help you to decode the menu. These cooking and menu terms are for understanding only, not for speaking aloud.

Cooking and menu terms

Kǎo yā	烤鸭	Peking duck
Jiàng bào ròu dīng	酱爆肉丁	Soy cooked pork
Sōng shǔ huáng yú	松鼠黄鱼	Yellow croaker
Chǎo sān yàng	炒三样	Fried liver and kidney
Xī hóng shì chǎo jī dàn	西红柿炒鸡蛋	Scrambled egg with tomato
Gàn shāo wán zi	干烧丸子	Dry fried meatballs
Dòu bàn guì yú	豆瓣桂鱼	fish in broad bean sauce
Gōng bào jī dīng	宫保鸡丁	Chicken with chili and nuts
Gǔ lǎo ròu	古老肉	Sweet-sour pork
Yú xiāng ròu sì	鱼香肉丝	Pork in sea-spiced sauce
Shāo qié zi	烧茄子	Stewed aubergine
Má pó dòu fǔ	麻婆豆腐	Spicy beancurd
Jiā chán dòu fǔ	家产豆腐	Home-style beancurd
Shí jǐn pīn pán	什锦拼盘	Mixed hors d'œuvres
Bá sī píng guǒ	拨丝苹果	Toffee apples
Bā bǎo fàn	八宝饭	Eight treasure rice
Suān là tāng	酸辣汤	Spicy-sour soup
Wán zi tāng	丸子汤	Meatball soup
Chǎo bō cài	炒菠菜	Stir-fried spinach
Shuàn yáng ròu	涮羊肉	Mongolian hot-pot
Mù xī ròu	木樨肉	Shredded pork with mushroom and scrambled egg

Chā shāo ròu	义烧肉	Pork in barbecue sauce
Huí guō ròu	回锅肉	Spicy twice-cooked pork
Xiāng sū jī	香酥鸡	Crispy fried chicken
Kǎo yáng ròu chuàn	烤羊肉串	Lamb kebabs
Jiāng bào jī dīng	酱爆鸡丁	Soy-cooked chicken
Cù là yú	醋椒鱼	Sour, spicy fish
Pí pa dà xiā	琵琶大虾	Pipa king prawns
Xiù qiú gān bèi	绣球干贝	Scallops
Lì zhī yóu yú	荔枝鱿鱼	Cuttle fish with litchi
Bàng bang jī	棒棒鸡	Bangbang chicken
Táng cù pái gǔ	糖醋排骨	Sweet and sour pork ribs
Fú róng hǎi shēn	芙蓉海参	Sea cucumber
Liáng miàn	凉面	Cold noodles
Dàn dàn miàn	担担面	Noodles with chili and meat
Chǎo miàn	炒面	Fried noodles (chow mien)
Jiā lǐ jī	咖喱鸡	Curried chicken
Mǎ yǐ shàng shù	蚂蚁上树	Vermicelli with meat
Pídan	皮蛋	1000 year old eggs
Dàn huā tāng	蛋花汤	Broth with egg
Báimǐ	白米	
Dàmǐ	大米	Rice
Mǐfàn	米饭	
Fàn	饭	
Chǎofàn	炒饭	Fried rice

Health

ESSENTIAL INFORMATION

- There is no general reciprocal health agreement between Britain and China. It is essential to take out medical insurance before travelling in China.
- Take your own 'first line' first aid kit with you. For minor disorders and treatment at a chemist's, see p.43.
- For asking the way to the doctor, dentist, or chemist, see p.23.

- Once in China, decide on a definite plan of action in case of serious illness; communicate your problem to a near neighbour, the receptionist or someone you see regularly. You are then dependent on that person helping you obtain treatment.
- To find a doctor in an emergency, ask for:

YÍYUÀN	医院	(hospital)
ZHĚNSUǑ	诊所	(clinic)
ZHĚNLIÁOSHÌ	诊疗室	(consulting room)
ZHŌNGYĪ YUÀN	中医院	(hospital of Chinese medicine)
XĪYĪ YUÀN	西医院	(hospital of Western medicine)

WHAT'S THE MATTER?

I have a pain in my ...
    Wǒ ... téng
    Waw ... tung
    我... 疼

ankle	**huái**	hwai / 踝
arm	**gēbo**	gu-bo / 胳膊
back (spine)	**bèi**	bay / 背
back (waist)	**yāo**	yaow / 腰
bladder	**niàodào**	nyaow-daow / 尿道
bowels	**gāngmén**	gang-min / 肛门
breast	**rǔfáng**	roo-fang / 乳房
chest	**xiōng**	syoong / 胸
ear	**ěrduo**	urr-dwo / 耳朵

eye	**yǎnjīng**	
	yen-jeeng	
	眼睛	
foot	**jiǎo**	
	jyaow	
	脚	
head	**tóu**	
	tow	
	头	
heel	**jiǎogēn**	
	jyaow-gin	
	脚跟	
jaw	**xiàba**	
	sya-ba	
	下巴	
kidney	**shèn**	
	shin	
	肾	
leg	**tuǐ**	
	tway	
	腿	
lung	**fèi**	
	fay	
	肺	
neck	**bózi**	
	bo-dz	
	脖子	
penis	**yīnjīng**	
	een-jeeng	
	阳茎	
shoulder	**jiān**	
	jyenn	
	肩	
stomach	**wèi**	
	way	
	胃	
testicle	**gāowán**	
	gaow-wan	
	睾丸	
throat	**hóulóng**	
	how-loong	
	喉咙	
vagina	**yīndào**	
	yeen-daow	
	阴道	

wrist	**shǒuwànzi** show-wan-dz 手腕子
I have a pain here (*point*)	**Wǒ zhèr téng** Waw jurr tung 我这儿疼
I have a toothache	**Wǒ yá téng** Waw ya tung 我牙疼
I have broken my false teeth	**Jiǎyá huàile** Jya-ya hwai-la 假牙坏了
I have broken my glasses	**Yǎnjìng huàile** Yen-jeeng hwai-la 眼镜坏了
I have lost my contact lens	**Wǒ diūle yǐnxíng yǎnjìng** Waw dyoo-la yeen-sing yenn-jeeng 我去了隐形眼镜
I have lost a filling	**Wǒ shànghuí bǔ yále, xiànzài diūle** Waw shang-hway boo ya-le, syenn-dzigh dyoo-la 我上回补牙了，现在丢了
My child is ill	**Wǒ háizi bìngle** Waw high-dz beeng-la 我孩子病了
He/she has a pain ...	**Tā ... téng** Ta ... tung 他...疼

[*For parts of the body, see list above*]

How bad is it?

I'm ill	**Wǒ bìngle** Waw beeng-la 我病了
It's urgent	**Hěn jí** Hin jee 很急
It's serious	**Hěn yánzhòng** Hin yen-joong 很严重

It's not serious	**Bù yánzhòng**
	Boo yen-joong
	不严重
It hurts	**Téng**
	Tung
	疼
It hurts a lot	**Téngde lìhai**
	Tung-de lee-high
	疼得利害
It doesn't hurt much	**Bù zénme téng**
	Boo dzumma tung
	不怎么疼
The pain occurs ...	**... téng yī cì**
	... tung ee tse
	....疼一次
every 15 minutes	**Měi shíwǔ fēnzhong**
	May shi-woo fin-joong
	每十五分钟
every half hour	**Měi bàn xiǎo shí**
	May ban syao shir
	每半小时
every hour	**Měi ge zhōngtóu**
	May ga joong-tow
	每个钟头
every day	**Měi tiān**
	May tyenn
	每天
It hurts most of the time	**Lǎo téng**
	Laow tung
	老疼
I've had it for ...	**Wǒ zhèiyàng yǒu ...**
	Waw jay-yang yow ...
	我这样有...
one hour/one day	**yī xiǎoshí/yī tiān**
	ee syao-shir/ee tyenn
	..小时／一天
two hours/two days	**liǎng xiǎoshí/liǎng tiān**
	lyang syao-shir/lyang tyenn
	两小时／两天
It's a sharp pain	**Shì ruì téng**
	Shir rway tung
	是锐疼
It's a dull ache	**Shì dùn téng**
	Shir doon tung
	是钝疼

It's a nagging pain	**Shì yǐn téng** Shir yeen tung 是隐疼
I feel ...	**Wǒ juéde ...** Waw jway-de 我觉得...
weak	**xū** su 虚
dizzy	**tóu yūn** tow yun 头晕
sick	**xiǎng tù** syang too 想吐
I am feverish	**Wǒ fāshāole** Waw fa-shaow-le 我发烧了
I don't have a fever	**Wǒ méi fāshāo** Waw may fa-shaow 我没发烧
I am bleeding	**Wǒ chū xuè le** Waw choo sway la 我出血了

Already under treatment for something else?

I take ... regularly [chow]	**Jīngcháng chī ...** Jeeng-chang chir ... 经常吃
this medicine	**zhè ge yào** jur ga yaow 这个药
these pills	**zhè zhòng yàopiàn** jay joong yaow-pyenn 这种药片
I have a heart condition	**Wǒ yǒu xīnzàng bìng** Waw yow seen-dzang bing 我有心脏病
I have haemorrhoids	**Wǒ yǒu zhì chuāng** Waw yow jir chwang 我有痔疮

I have rheumatism	**Wǒ yǒu fēng shī bìng**
	Waw yow fung shir bing
	我有风湿病
I'm diabetic	**Wǒ yǒu tángniào bìng**
	Waw yow tang-neeaow-beeng
	我有糖尿病
I'm asthmatic	**Wǒ yǒu xiàochuǎn**
	Waw yow syaow-chwann
	我有哮喘
I'm pregnant	**Wǒ huáiyùnle**
	Waw hwai-yoon-la
	我怀孕了
I'm allergic to penicillin	**Wǒ duì pánníxīlín guòmǐn**
	Waw dway pan-nee-see-leen
	gwo-meen
	我对盘尼西林过敏

Other essential expressions

Please can you help?	**Néng bāng wǒ ma?**
	Nung bang waw ma
	能帮我吗?
A doctor, please	**Qǐng zhǎo dàifu**
	Cheeng jaow digh-foo
	请找大夫
I can't speak Chinese	**Wǒ bù huí Zhōngwén**
	Waw boo hway Joong-win
	我不会中文
What time does ... arrive?	**... shénme shíhou lái?**
	... shumma shi-how lye
	...什么时候来?
the doctor	**Dàifu**
	Digh-foo
	大夫
the dentist	**Yáyī**
	Ya-yee
	牙医

From the doctor: key sentences to understand

Take this every day/hour	**Měitiān/měi xiǎoshí chī yīcì**
	May-tyenn/may syao-shir chir
	ee-tsi
	每天／每小时吃一次
Take this twice/four times a day	**Měitiān chī liǎngcì/sìcì**
	May-tyenn chir lyang-tsi/si-tsi
	每天吃两次／四次

Stay in bed	**Wòchuáng** Waw-chwang 卧床
Don't travel for ... days	**Děng ... tiān cái néng jìxù lǚxíng** Dung ... tyenn tsigh nung jee-soo loo-sing 等...天才能继续旅行
You must go to hospital	**Nǐ yídìng děi shàng yīyuàn** Nee ee-ding day shang ee-ywann 你一定得上医院

Problems: complaints, loss, theft

ESSENTIAL INFORMATION

- Problems with: health, see p.43
household appliances, see p.17   the car, see p.108
- If the worst comes to the worst, ask for the police or for your embassy or consulate.
- To ask the way, see p.23
Look for:
RÉNMÍN JĬNGCHÁ   (People's policeman)   人民警察
JĬNGCHÁJÚ   (Police station)   警察局
SHĬGUĂN   (Embassy)   使馆
- If you lose your passport or other travel documents, contact the British Embassy, Consulate or representative.
- Ask a friend or neighbour to help you in an emergency.

COMPLAINTS

I bought this ...	**... mǎi zhèige** ... mye jay-ga 买这个
today	**Jīntiān** Jeen-tyenn 今天
yesterday	**Zuótiān** Dzo-tyenn 昨天

on Monday (see p.136)	**Xīngqīyī** Seeng-chee-ee 星期一
It's no good	**Bù hǎo** Boo haow 不好
Look	**Kàn ba** Kan-ba 看吧
Here [*point*]	**Zhèr** Jerr 这儿
Can you ...	**Néng ...** Nung ... 能...
change it?	**huàn ma?** whann ma 换吗?
mend it?	**xiūlǐ ma?** syoo-lee ma 修理吗?
give me a refund?	**guīhuán qián ma?** gway-hwann chyenn ma 归还钱吗?
Here's the receipt	**Zhèi shì shōujù** Jay shi shou-joo 这是收据
Can I see the manager?	**Wǒ kàn jīnglǐ ba?** Waw kann jeeng-lee ba 我看经理吧

LOSS
[*See also 'Theft' below; the lists are interchangeable*]

I have lost ...	**Wǒ diūle ...** Waw dyoo-la ... 我丢了...
my bag	**shǒutíbāo** show-tee-baow 手提包
my camera	**zhàoxiàngjī** jaow-syang-jee 照相机
my car keys	**qìchē yàoshi** chee-chuh yaow-shr 汽车钥匙

my car logbook	**qìchē rìlì**
	chee-chuh ri-lee
	汽车日历
my driving licence	**kāichē zhèng**
	kigh-chuh jung
	开车证
my insurance certificate	**bǎoxiǎn zhèng**
	baow-syenn jung
	保险证
my jewellery	**zhūbǎo**
	jew-baow
	珠宝
everything	**yīqié**
	ee-chye
	一切

THEFT

[See also 'Loss' above; the lists are interchangeable]

Someone has stolen ...	**Rénjia tōule ...**
	Rin-jya tow-la ...
	人家偷了
my car	**wǒ qìchē**
	waw chee-chuh
	我汽车
my car radio	**qìchē shōuyīnjī**
	chee-chuh shou-yeen-ji
	汽车收音机
my keys	**wǒde yàoshi**
	wo-de yaow-shr
	我的钥匙
my luggage	**xíngli**
	seeng-lee
	行李
my money	**wǒ de qián**
	waw di chyenn
	我的钱
my necklace	**wǒ de xiàngquān**
	waw di syang-chwann
	我的项圈
my passport	**wǒ hùzhào**
	waw hoo-jaow
	我护照
my purse	**wǒ qiánbāo**
	waw chyenn-baow
	我钱包

my radio	**shōuyīnjī**
	show-yeen-jee
	收音机
my tickets	**wǒde piào**
	waw-di pyao
	我的票
my traveller's cheques	**wǒde lǚyóu zhīpiào**
	waw-di lu-yow jir-pyaow
	我的旅行支票
my wallet	**wǒ pí jiāzi**
	waw pee jya-dz
	我皮夹子
my watch	**wǒ shǒubiǎo**
	waw show-byaow
	我手表

LIKELY REACTIONS: key words to understand

Wait	**Děng**
	Dung
	等
When?	**Shénme shíhou?**
	Shumma shi-how
	什么时候?
Where?	**Zài nǎr?**
	Dzigh narr
	在哪儿?
Name (Surname, given name)?	**Xìngmíng**
	Seeng-meeng
	姓名
Address?	**Dìzhǐ?**
	Dee-jir
	地址
I can't help you	**Bù néng bāng ni**
	Boo nung bang nee
	不能帮你
There's nothing to be done	**Méiyǒu bànfǎ**
	May-yow ban-far
	没有办法
Nothing to do with me	**Bùshì wǒde shì**
	Boo-shi waw-di shr
	不是我的事

The post office

ESSENTIAL INFORMATION

- To find a post office, see p.23
- Key words to look for:
  - YÓUJÚ (Post office) 邮局
  - YÓUZHÈNGJÚ (Post office) 邮政局
  - DIÀNBÀO (Telegrams) 电报
- Stamps are also sold in hotels catering for foreigners.
- Don't wrap your parcels before taking them to the Post Office. Take string, tape and glue with you and wrap up under the supervision of the clerk after the contents have been examined.
- Chinese envelopes and stamps are not gummed. A glue stick is useful, or use the pot of glue found in any post office.
- For stamps look for the word YÓUPIÀO. 邮票
- Letter boxes are green and yellow.

WHAT TO SAY

To England, please
[*Hand letters, cards or parcels over the counter*]
Qǐng jìwǎng Yīngguó
Cheeng jee-wang Eeng-gwo
请寄往英国

To Australia
Jì Àodàlìyà
Jee Aow-da-lee-ya
寄澳大利亚

To the United States
Jì Měiguó
Jee May-gwo
寄美国

[*For other countries, see p.142*]

How much is ...
... duōshǎo qián?
... dwo-shaow chyenn
...多少钱?

this parcel to Canada?
Zhèi bāo jì Jiānádà
Jay baow jee Jya-na-da
这包寄加拿大

a letter to Australia?
Xìnfēng jì Àodàlìyà
Seen-fung jee Aow-da-lee-ya
信封寄澳大利亚

a postcard to England?
Míngxìnpiàn jì Yīngguó
Moong-soon-pyenn jee Eeng-gwo
明心片寄英国

Air mail	**Hángkōng** Hang koong 航空
Registered	**Guàhaò** Gwa-how 挂号
Surface mail	**Pǔtōng yóujiàn** Poo-toong yow-jyenn 普通邮件
One stamp, please	**Mǎi yīzhāng yóupiào** Mye ee-jang yow-pyaow 买一长邮票
Two stamps	**Liǎngzhāng yóupiào** lyang-jang yow-pyao 两长邮票
One 1Y50 stamp	**Yīzhāng yīkuàiwǔ de** Ee-jang ee-kwai-woo de 一长一块五的

Telephoning

ESSENTIAL INFORMATION

WHAT TO SAY

Where can I make a telephone call?	**Zài nǎr dǎ diànhuà?** Dzye narr da dyenn-hwa 在哪儿打电话?
Local/abroad	**Guónèi/Guówài** Gwo-nay/Gwo-wye 国内/国外
I'd like this number ... (*show number*)	**Yào zhèi hàomǎ** Yaow jay how-ma 要这号码
in England	**zài Yīngguó** dzigh Eeng-gwo 在英国
in Canada	**zài Jiānádà** dzigh Jya-na-da 在加拿大

in the USA	**zài Měiguó**
[*For other countries, see p.142*]	dzigh May-gwo
	在美国
Can you dial it for me, please?	**Qǐng gěi wǒ bō hàomǎ**
	Cheeng gay waw baw how-ma
	请给我拨号码
How much is it?	**Duōshǎo qián?**
	Dwo-shaow chyenn
	多少钱?
Hello?	**Wèi?**
	Way
	喂?
May I speak to ...?	**Qǐng zhǎo ...?**
	Cheeng jaow ...
	请找?
Extension ...	**... fēnxiàn**
	... fin-syenn
	...分线
I'm sorry I don't speak Chinese	**Bàoqiàn, bùhuí Zhōngwén**
	Bow-chyenn, boo-hway Joong-win
	抱歉，不会中文
Do you speak English?	**Nǐ huí Yīngwén ma?**
	Nee whay Eeng-wen ma
	你会英文吗?
Thank you, I'll phone back	**Xièxie, yīhuí zài dǎ**
	Sye-sye, ee-whey dzigh da
	谢谢，一回再打
Goodbye	**Zàijiàn!**
	Dzye-jyenn!
	再见!

LIKELY REACTIONS

That's ...	**Shì ...**
	Shr ...
	是
Cabin number (3)	**Dì (sān) diànhuà jiàn**
[*For numbers, see p.128*	Dee (san) dyenn-hwa jyenn
	第(三)电话间
Don't hang up	**Bùyào duànxiàn**
	Boo-yaow dwann-syenn
	不要断线
I'm trying to connect you	**Kuài yào jiēxiàn**
	Kwai yaow jye-syenn
	快要接线

You're through	**Dǎtōngle** Da-tong-le 打通了
There's a delay	**Shāowēi děngyiděng** Shaow-way dung-ee-dung 稍微等一等
The number is engaged	**Zhànxiànle** Jan-syenn-la 占线了
I'll try again	**Wǒ zài shìshi** Wo dzigh shr-shr 我再试试
I want to send a telex	**Xiǎng dǎ diàn chuán** Syang da dyenn chwan 想打电传
I want to send a cable	**Xiǎng dǎ diàn bào** Syang da dyenn baow 想打电报
I want to send a fax	**Xiǎng dǎ túwén chuán zhēn** Syang da too-win chwan-jinn 想打图文传真
Do you have a telephone directory?	**Yǒu diànhuà bú ma?** You dyenn-hwa boo ma 有电话薄吗?

Travelers' checks and money

ESSENTIAL INFORMATION

- For finding the way to the bank or exchange bureau, see p.23.
- Look for these words on buildings:

YÍNHÁNG	(Bank)	银行
ZHŌNGGUÓ YÍNHÁNG	(Bank of China)	中国银行
ZHŌNGGUÓ RÉNMÍN YÍNHÁNG	(People's Bank of China)	中国人民银行
HUÀNQIÁN	(Change money)	换钱

- It is best to travel with travellers' cheques, which are readily exchanged in the bank or in major hotels in most big towns. Credit cards are accepted in a few places in the biggest cities

but terms and usage vary and it is best not to rely on credit cards if you want to travel in remoter parts of the country.

● Have your passport ready and be prepared to show receipts for your exchanged money when leaving the country. There is a complicated system of Foreign Exchange Certificates (FECs, Wàihuìquàn 外汇券) which in essence means that your hard currency is changed for a Chinese hard currency. If you change money or FECs on the black market, you will have problems on leaving China unless you have spent all your Renminbi (People's Currency). It is forbidden to export Renminbi from China and it is also impossible to change it back into foreign currency.

WHAT TO SAY

I'd like to change	**Wǒ xiǎng huàn ...** Waw syang hwann ... 我想换
this travellers' cheque	**lǔxíng zhīpiào** loo-seeng jir-piaow 旅行支票
this cheque	**zhīpiào** jir-piaow 支票
I'd like to change this into Renminbi/FEC	**Xiǎng huàn Rénmínbì/ Wàihuìquàn** Syang hwann Rin-min-bee/ Wye-hway-chwan 想换人民币／外汇券
Here's ...	**Zhèi shì ...** Jay shir ... 这是...
my credit card	**xìnyòng kǎ** seen-yoong ka 信用卡
my passport	**hùzhào** hoo-jaow 护照

For travel on into neighbouring countries
(*show bank notes*)

I'd like to change this ...	**Xiǎng huàn ...** Syang hwan ... 想换...

into Hong Kong dollars	**Găngbì** Gang-bee 港币
into Japanese yen	**Rìyuán** Rih-ywann 日元
into Thai bhat	**Tài zhū** Tie-jew 泰铢
into Russian roubles	**Lúbù** Lou-boo 卢布
into Mongolian Tugrik	**Měnggǔ Túgélìkè** Mung-goo Too-ge-lee-ko 蒙古图格里克
into US dollars	**Měi yuán** May-ywann 美元
What's the exchange rate for dollars/pounds?	**Huàn duōshǎo qián yī yuán/ bàng?** Hwann daw-shaow chyenn ee ywann/bang 换多少钱一元/一镑?

LIKELY REACTIONS

Passport, please	**Qǐng ná hùzhào** Cheeng na hoo-jaow 请拿护照
Sign here	**Qǐng qiān míng** Cheeng chyenn meeng 请签名
Your credit card, please	**Qǐng ná xìnyòng kǎ** Cheeng na seen-yoong ka 请拿信用卡
Go to the cash desk	**Qǐng dào shōukuǎntái qù** Cheeng daow show-kwann-tigh chew 请到收款台去

Car travel

ESSENTIAL INFORMATION

- For finding a filling station or garage, see p.23.
- There are no self-service petrol stations in China.
- For all practical purposes, the only grade used is standard.
- 1 gallon is about 4½ litres (accurate up to about 6 gallons).
- Petrol stations do not service and repair vehicles. For this you must find a 汽车维修站 Qìchē wéixiū zhàn.
- You must have an international driving licence.
- There are no 'car hire' companies. If you want to drive in China, enquire before finalizing your plans. You may have to engage a Chinese driver.
- Driving under the influence of alcohol is forbidden. Parking in large cities is troublesome but not expensive. China drives on the right. Road signs are international but other signs giving names of places, exits, etc. are mostly in Chinese.
- Driving at night is disconcerting. You must keep sidelights on, except when another vehicle approaches, when you should dip your headlights. Watch out for bicycles without lamps.

WHAT TO SAY
[*For numbers, see p.128*]

(9) litres of petrol	**(Jiǔ) shēng qìyóu** (Jew) shung chee-yow （九）升汽油
(50) yuan of petrol	**(Wǔshí) kuài qìyóu** (Woo-shi) kwigh chee-yow （五十）块汽油
Diesel	**cháiyóu** chigh-yow 柴油
Fill it up, please	**Qǐng guàn mǎn** Cheeng gwan-man 请灌满
Will you check ...	**Qǐng nǐ jiǎnchá ...** Cheeng nee jyenn-cha 请你检查…
the oil	**yóu** yow 油

the battery	**xù diànchí**
	soo dyenn-chir
	蓄电池
the radiator	**sànrèqì**
	san-ruh-chee
	散热器
the tyres	**lúntāi**
	loon-tigh
	轮胎
I've run out of petrol	**Wǒde qìyóu yòngwánle**
	Waw-di chee-yow yoong-wan-la
	我的汽油用完了
Can I borrow a can?	**Kěyǐ jiè yī guàn ma?**
	Ko-ee jye ee gwann ma
	可以借 一罐吗?
My car has broken down	**Wǒde chē huàile**
	Waw-di chuh why-la
	我的车坏了
My car won't start	**Wǒde chē fādòngbùliǎo**
	Waw-di chuh fa-doong boo-lyaow
	我的车发动不了
I've had an accident	**Wǒ chū shìgù le**
	Waw choo shi-goo la
	我出事故了
I've lost my car keys	**Wǒ bǎ chē yàoshi diūle**
	Waw ba chuh yaow-shir dyoo-la
	我把车钥匙丢了
My car is ...	**Wǒ de chē zài ...**
	Waw-di chuh dzye ...
	我的车在...
one km away	**yī gōnglǐ wài**
	ee goonglee wigh
	一公里外
three km away	**sān gōnglǐ wài**
	san goonglee wigh
	三公里外
Can you help me, please?	**Néng bāng wǒ ma?**
	Nung bang waw ma?
	能帮我吗?
Do you do repairs?	**Néng xiūlǐ ma?**
	Nung syoo-lee ma?
	能修理吗?
I have a puncture	**Wǒde lúntāi bèi cǐpòle**
	Waw-di loon-tigh bay tsi-paw-la
	我的轮胎被刺破了

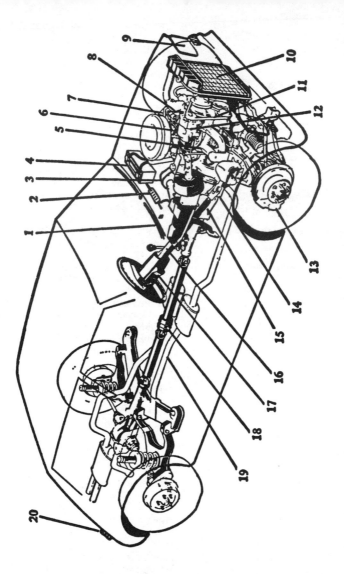

No.	English	Pinyin	Pronunciation	Chinese
1	windscreen wipers	**guāshuǐ qì**	gwa-shway chee	刮水器
2	fuses	**bǎoxiǎn sī**	baow-syenn-ssi	保险丝
3	heater	**jiā rè qì**	jya ruh chee	加热器
4	battery	**xù diàn chí**	soo dyenn chir	蓄电池
5	engine	**yǐn qíng**	yeen cheeng	引擎
6	fuel pump	**ránliào bèng**	ran-lyaow bung	燃料泵
7	starter motor	**qǐ dòng qì**	chee doong chee	起动器
8	carburettor	**qì huà qì**	chee wha chee	汽化器
9	lights	**zhào míng dēng**	jaow ming dung	照明灯
10	radiator	**sàn rè qì**	san ruh chee	散热器
11	fan belt	**gǔ fēng jī pí dài**	goo fung jee pee dye	鼓风机皮带
12	generator	**fā dòng jī**	fa doong jee	发动机
13	brakes	**zhì dòng qì**	jih doong chee	制动器
14	clutch	**lí hé qì**	lee ho chee	离合器
15	gear box	**biàn sù xiāng**	byenn soo syang	变速箱
16	steering wheel	**fāng xiàng pán**	fang syang pan	方向盘
17	ignition	**fā huǒ zhuāng zhì**	fa hwo jwang jir	发火装置
18	transmission	**biàn sù qì**	byenn soo chee	变速器
19	exhaust	**pái qì tǒng**	pigh chee toong	排气筒
20	indicators	**zhǐ shì qì**	jih shir chee	指示器

I have a broken windscreen	**Wǒde dǎngfēng bōlí pòle** Waw-di dang-fung baw-lee paw la 我的挡风玻璃破了
I don't know what's wrong	**Wǒ bù zhīdào nǎli huàile** Waw boo jir-daow na-lee hwigh-la 我不知道哪里坏了
I think the problem is here ...	**Wǒ kàn wèntí zài zhèr** Waw kan win-tee dzigh jurr 我看问题在这儿
Can you ...	**Nǐ néng ...** Nee nung ... 你能...
repair the fault?	**xiū zhè máobìng ma?** syoo juh maow-bing ma 修这毛病吗?
come and look?	**lái kànkan ma?** ligh kan-kan ma 来看看吗?
estimate the cost?	**gūjī fèiyòng ma?** goo-jee fay-yoong ma 诂计费用吗?
Can you write it down?	**Nǐ néng xiěxiàlái ma?** Nee nung sye-sya-ligh ma 你能写下来吗?
How long will the repair take?	**Xiūlǐ yào duōcháng shíjiān?** Syoolee yaow dwo-chang shi-jyenn 修理要多长时间?
When will the car be ready?	**Chē shénme shíhou néng xiūhǎo?** Chuh shumma shi-how nung syoo-haow 车什么时候能修好?
This is my insurance document	**Zhè shì bǎoxiǎn zhèngshū** Jay shir baowsyenn jungshoo 这是我的保险证书

HIRING A CAR

Can I hire a car?	**Kěyǐ zū chē ma?** Ko-yee dzoo chuh ma 可以租车吗?
I need a car for two people	**Yào liǎngrén yòngde chē** Yaow lyang-rin yoong-d chuh 要两人用的车

I need a car for five people	**Yào wǔrén yòngde chē**
	Yaow woo-rin yoong-d chuh
	要五人用的车
I want it for a day	**Yòng yītiān**
	Yoong ee-tyenn
	用一天
I want it for five days	**Yòng wǔtiān**
	Yoong woo-tyenn
	用五天
I want it for a week	**Yòng yī zhōu**
	Yoong ee jow
	用一周
Can you write down?	**Nǐ néng xiěxià ...**
	Nee nung sye-sya ...
	你能写下...
the deposit to pay	**yào xián fù duōshǎo qián?**
	yaow syenn foo dwo-shaow
	chyenn
	要先付多少钱?
the charge per km	**měi gōnglǐ fèiyòng**
	may goong-lee fay yoong
	每公里费用
the daily charge	**měitiān fèiyòng**
	may-tyenn fay-yoong
	每天费用
the insurance cost	**bǎoxiǎnfèi**
	baow-syenn-fay
	保险费
Can I leave it in (Canton)?	**Wǒ néng bǎ ta fàng zài**
	(Guǎngzhōu) ma?
	Waw nung ba ta fang dzigh
	(Gwang-jow) ma
	我能把它放在(广州)吗?
What documents do I need?	**Wǒ xūyào shénme zhèngjiàn?**
	Waw soo-yaow shumma jung-
	jyenn
	我需要什么证件?

LIKELY REACTIONS

I don't do repairs	**Wǒ bù xiūlǐ**
	Waw boo syoo-lee
	我不修理

Where's your car?	**Nǐde chē zài nǎr?** Nee-d chuh dzigh narr 你的车在哪儿?
What make is it?	**Shí shénme pái?** Shi shumma pigh 是人么牌?
Come back tomorrow	**Míngtiān lái** Meeng-tyenn ligh 明天来
Come back on Monday [*For days of the week, see p.136*]	**Xīngqīyī lái** Seeng-chee-yee ligh 星期一来
We don't hire cars	**Wǒmen bù zū chē** Wo-men boo dzoo chuh 我们不租车
Your driving licence, please	**Qǐng ná nǐde jiàshǐ zhízhào** Cheeng na nee-d jya-shir jih-jaow 请拿你的驾驶执照
The mileage is unlimited	**Lǐshù bù xiàn** Lee-shoo boo syenn 哩数不限

Public transportation

ESSENTIAL INFORMATION

- For finding the way to the bus station, a bus stop, railway station and taxi rank, see p.23.
- Using the public bus system is often the only alternative to expensive taxis. There is an underground railway in Beijing and one in Hong Kong. If you are at all unsure of your directions, carry a piece of paper with the name of your destination written in Chinese characters. Show it to the conductor or someone in the crowd and ask them to help you.
- Buying train tickets is complicated: there are different fares for foreigners and Chinese, and different rates for different categories of foreigners. If you want to save money, ask a Chinese friend to buy your ticket, or show your student card. If you want to save time and nervous energy, let China International Travel Service buy your ticket at the foreigners' rate.

- Distances in China are enormous. If in doubt, don't skimp on sleeper accommodation. Internal flights are often overbooked and getting on a plane can involve endless waiting around airports. Coastal and river ferries are well worth taking.
- Key words on signs:

ZHŌNGGUÓ TIĚLÙ	Chinese Railways	中国铁路
TÈ KUÀI CHĒ	Express Train	特快车
KUÀICHĒ	Fast Train	快车
MÀNCHĒ	Slow Train	慢车
DÌXIÀ TIĚ LÙ	Underground railway	地下铁道
SHÒU PIÀOCHÙ	ticket sales	售票处
GŌNG GÒNG QÌ CHĒ	bus	公共汽车
CHŪZŪ QÌCHĒ	taxi	出租汽车
LÚNCHUÁN	steamship	轮船

WHAT TO SAY

Where do I buy a ticket?

Piào zài nǎr mǎi?
Pyaow dzigh narr migh
票在哪儿买?

When does the train for (Shanghai) leave?

Qù (Shànghǎi) de huǒchē jǐdiǎn kāi?
Choo (Shang-hai) de hwo-chuh jee-dyenn kigh
去(上海)的火车几点开?

When does the train arrive in (Shanghai)?

Huǒchē jǐdiǎn dào (Shànghǎi)?
Hwo-chuh jee-dyenn daow (Chang-hai)?
火车几点到(上海)?

Is this the boat for Shanghai?

Zhèi shì qù Shànghǎi de lúnchuán ma?
Jay shi choo Shang-high di loon-chwan ma
这是去上海的轮船吗?

Where does the bus for Wuxi leave from?

Qù Wúxī de gōnggòng qìchē cóng nǎr kāi?
Choo Woo-see de goong-goong chee-chuh tsoong narr kigh
去(无锡)的公共汽车从哪儿开?

When does the bus leave for Wuxi?

Qù Wúxī de gōnggòng qìchē jǐdiǎn kāi?
Choo Woo-see de goong-goong chee-chuh jee-dyenn kigh
去(无锡)的公共汽车几点开?

Is this the bus for (Wuxi)?

Zhèi chē qù (Wúxī) ma?
Jay chuh choo (Woo-see) ma
这车去 (无锡) 吗?

Do I have to change?

Yào bù yào huàn chē?
Yaow boo yaow hwan chuh
要不要换车?

Where does the bus for ... leave from?

Qù ... de gōnggòng qìchē cóng nǎr kāi?
Choo ... de goong-goong chee-chuh tsoong narr kigh
去...的公共汽车从哪儿开?

the airport

fēijī chǎng
fay-jee-chang
飞机厂

the beach

hǎibīn
high-been
海滨

the market place

shìchǎng
shi-chang
市场

the railway station

huǒchē zhàn
hwo-chuh jann
火车站

the town centre

chénglǐ
chung-lee
成里

the town hall

zhèngfǔ bàngōng lóu
jung-foo ban-goong low
政府办公楼

the Confucius temple

Kǒng miào
Koong myaow
孔庙

the swimming pool

yóuyǒng chí
yow-yoong chi
游泳池

Is this ...

Zhèi shì bù shì ...
Jay shi boo shi
这是不是...

the bus for the town?

qù chénglǐ de gōnggòng qìchē?
choo chung-lee de goong-goong chee-chuh
去成里的公共汽车?

the bus for the airport?	**qù jīchǎng de gōnggòng qìchē?** choo jee-chang di goong-goong chee-chuh 去机厂的公共汽车?
Where can I get a taxi?	**Chūzū qìchē zài nǎr?** Choo-dzoo chee-chuh dzigh narr 出租汽车在哪儿?
Can you put me off at the right stop, please?	**Dào xià chē nèi zhàn, qǐng gàosu wǒ** Daow sya chuh nay jann, cheeng gaow-soo waw 到下车那站, 请告诉我
Can I book a seat?	**Kěyǐ dìng zuòwei ma?** Ko-ee ding dzo-way ma 可以订坐位吗?
Can I book a berth?	**Kěyǐ dìng wòpù ma?** Ko-ee ding waw-poo ma 可以订卧铺吗?
A single	**Dānchéng piào** Dan-chung pyaow 单程票
A return	**Láihuí piào** Ligh-hway piaow 来回票
First (soft) class seat/berth	**Ruǎnzuò/wò** Rwann-dzo/waw 软坐／卧
Second (hard) class seat/berth	**Yìngzuò/wò** Yeeng-dzo/waw 硬坐／卧

Note: 席 xí/see is an alternative word for seat
e.g. 软席 ruǎnxí

One adult	**yīge chéngnián rén** ee-ga chung-nyenn ren 一个成年人
Two adults	**liǎngge chéngnián rén** lyang-ga chung-nyenn ren 两个成年人
and one child	**háiyǒu yīge háizi** high-yow ee-ga high-dz 还有一个孩子

and two children
[In China you pay for
children over one
metre tall]

liǎngge háizi
lyang-ga high-dz
两个孩子

How much is it?

Duōshǎo qián?
Daw-shaow chyenn
多少钱?

LIKELY REACTIONS

Over there

Nèibiàn
Nay-byenn
那边

Here

Zhèibian
Jay-byenn
这边

Platform (one)

Dì (yī) yuètái/zhàntái
Dee (yee) ywe-tigh/jan-tigh
第(一)月台／站台

At (four o'clock)

(Sì) diǎn zhōng
(Si) dyenn joong
(四)点钟

Change at (Xinjiekou)

Dào (Xīnjiēkǒu) huànchē
Daow (Seen-jye-kow) hwan-chuh
到(新街口)换车

Change at (the town hall)

Dào (zhèngfǔ bàngōnglóu) huànchē
Daow (jung-foo ban-goong-low) hwan-chuh
到(政府办公楼)换车

This is your stop

Xiànzài xià chē
Syenn-dzigh sya chuh
现在下车

There's only first class

Zhǐ yǒu ruǎn wò
Jih yow rwann waw
只有软卧

It's train number 27

Shì dì èrshíqī cì huǒchē
Shir dee urr-shi-chee tsi hwo-chuh
是第二十七次火车

Here is the timetable

Zhèi shì shíkè biǎo
Jay shi shi-ko-byow
这是时刻表

Leisure

ESSENTIAL INFORMATION

- For finding the way to a place of entertainment, see p.23.
- For times of day, see p.133.
- Important signs, see p.125.
- In Beijing, the *China Daily* carries details of entertainments. Elsewhere you will have to rely on Chinese friends or guides to recommend shows or places to visit.

WHAT TO SAY

At what time does ... open?	**... jǐdiǎn kāimén?**
	... jee-dyenn kigh men
	...几点开门?
the art gallery	**Měishùguǎn**
	May-shoo-gwan
	美术馆
the botanical garden	**Zhíwù yuán**
	Jih-woo-ywann
	植物园
the concert hall	**Yīnyuè táng**
	Yeen-yweh-tang
	音乐堂
the disco	**Dīsīkē**
	Dee-sı-ko
	迪斯科
the museum	**Bówùguǎn**
	Bo-woo-gwan
	博物馆
the night-club	**Yè zǒnghuì**
	Ye dzoong-hway
	夜总会
the sports stadium	**Tǐyù chǎng**
	Tee-yoo chang
	体育场
the swimming pool	**Yóuyǒng chí**
	Yow-yoong chih
	游泳池

the theatre	**Jùchǎng** Joo-chang 剧场
the zoo	**Dòngwùyuán** Doong-woo-ywann 动物园
At what time does ... close?	**... jǐdiǎn guānmén?** ... jee-dyenn gwan-men ...几点关门?
the art gallery [*see list above*]	**Měishùguǎn** May-shoo gwann 美术馆
At what time does ... start?	**... jǐdiǎn kāishǐ?** ... jee-dyenn kigh-shih ...几点开始?
the concert	**Yīnyuè huì** Yeen-ywe-hway 音乐会
the film	**Diànyǐng** Dyenn-yeeng 电影
the match	**Bǐsài** Bee-sigh 比赛
the play	**Huàjù** Hwa-joo 话剧
the race	**Sàipǎo** Sigh-paow 赛跑
How much is it ...	**... duōshǎo qián?** ... daw-shaow chyenn ...多少钱?
for an adult/a child?	**Chéngniánrén/háizi** Chung-nyenn-ren/high-dz 成年人／孩子
Two adults, please	**Liǎngge chéngniánrén** Lyang-ga chung-nyenn-ren 两个成年人
Three children, please [*Usually you pay for children over one metre tall*]	**Sānge háizi** Sann-ga high-dz 三个孩子

Do you have ...	**Yǒu méi yǒu ...**
	Yow may yow ...
	有没有...
a programme?	**jiémù dān?**
	jye-moo dan
	节目单？
a guide book?	**zhǐnán?**
	jih-nan
	指南
Where is the toilet, please?	**Qǐngwèn, cèsuǒ zài nǎr?**
	Cheeng-wen, tsuh-swo dzigh narr
	请问, 厕所在哪儿?
Where is the cloakroom?	**Yīmàojiān zài nǎr?**
	Ee-maow-jyenn dzigh narr
	衣帽间在哪儿?
I would like lessons in ...	**Wǒ xiǎng xué ...**
	Waw syang swe ...
	我想学...
sailing	**hángxíng**
	hang-seeng
	航行
skiing	**huáxuě**
	hwa-swe
	滑雪
water skiing	**yòng huáshuǐ qiāo**
	yoong hwa-shway chyaow
	用滑水橇
wind surfing	**fān bǎn**
	fan ban
	帆板
tai-ji- quan (shadow boxing)	**tàijíquán**
	tigh-jee-chwann
	太极拳
martial arts	**wǔshù**
	woo-shoo
	武术
Can I hire ...	**Kěyǐ zū ...**
	Ko-yee dzoo ...
	可以租...
a bicycle?	**zìxíngchē ma?**
	dzi-seeng-chuh ma
	自行车吗?

some skis?	**huáxuébǎn ma?** hwa-sweh-ban ma 滑雪板吗?
some ski-boots?	**huáxué xié ma?** hwa-swe sye ma 滑雪鞋吗?
a boat?	**chuán ma?** chwann ma 船吗?
a fishing rod?	**diàoyúgān ma?** dyow-yoo-gan ma 钓鱼竿吗?
the necessary equipment?	**bìyàode zhuāngbèi ma?** bee-yaow de jwang-bay ma 必要的装备吗?
How much is it ...	**... duōshǎo qián?** ... daw-shaow chyenn ...多少钱?
per day/per hour?	**Yītiān/yīge zhōngtóu** Ee-tyenn/eega joong-tow 一天／一个钟头
Do I need a licence?	**Xūyào zhèngmíngshū ma?** Soo-yaow jung-meeng shoo-ma 需要证明书吗?

Asking if things are allowed

WHAT TO SAY

Excuse me, please	**Láojià/Qǐngwèn** Laow-jya/Cheeng-win 劳驾，请问
May one ...	**Zhèr kěyǐ ... ma?** Jurr ko-yee ... ma 这儿可以...吗?
camp here?	**sùyíng** soo-ying 宿营
dance here?	**tiàowǔ** tyaow-woo 跳舞

fish here?	**diàoyú** dyaow-yoo 钓鱼
get out this way?	**chūlái** choo-ligh 出来
leave one's things here?	**fàng dōngxi** fang doong-see 放东西
look around?	**kànkan** kan-kan 看看
park here?	**tíngchē** teeng-chuh 停车
picnic here?	**qù yěcān** choo ye-tsan 去野餐
sit here?	**zuò yi zuò** dzo yee dzo 坐一坐
smoke here?	**chōuyān** chow-yenn 抽烟
swim here?	**yóuyǒng** yow-yoong 游泳
take photos here?	**zhàoxiàng** jaow-syang 照相
telephone here?	**dǎ diànhuà** da dyenn-hwa 打电话
wait here?	**děng** dung 等
May we come in?	**Kěyǐ jìnlái ma?** Ko-yee jeen-ligh ma 可以进来吗?

LIKELY REACTIONS

Yes, certainly	**Huānyíng** Hwan-yeeng 欢迎
Help yourself	**Zìjǐ lái** Dzi-jee ligh 自己来
I think so	**Hǎoxiàng shì** Haow-syang shir 好像是
Of course	**Dāngrán** Dang-ran 当然
It's not convenient	**Bù fāngbiàn** Boo fang-byenn 不方便
Yes, but be careful	**Hǎoba, zhùyì ānquán** Haow-ba, joo-ee ann-chwann 好吧, 注意安全
No, certainly not	**Bùxíng** Boo-seeng 不行
I don't think so	**Hǎoxiàng bùxíng** Haow-syang boo-seeng 好像不行
Not normally	**Yībànde bùxíng** Yee-ban-de boo-seeng 一般的不行
Sorry	**Bàoqiàn/duìbùqǐ** Baow-chyenn/dway-boo-chee 抱歉／对不起

Reference

SIGN LANGUAGE

- Key words on signs for drivers, pedestrians, travellers, shoppers and overnight guests.

CHUGUAN	出关	Departures
JINGUAN	进关	Arrivals
HAIGUAN	海关	Customs
JIEDAI	接待	Reception
DIANTI	电梯	Lift
ZIDONG DIANTI	自动楼梯	Escalator
RUKOU	入口	Entrance
CHUKOU	出口	Exit
JLJIN CHUKOU	紧急出口	Emergency exit
MIANFEI RUCHANG	免费入场	Admission free
GONGYONG DIANHUA	公用电话	Public telephone
TUI	推	Push
LA	拉	Pull
XIAOXIN	小心	Caution
JINZHI	禁止	Forbidden
BUZHUN RUNEI	不准入内	No trespassing
WUREN	无人	Vacant
SHIYONG ZHONG	使用中	Engaged
XISHOUJIAN/CESUO	洗手间／厕所	Toilet
GONGYONG CESUO	公用厕所	Public convenience
NÜ CESUO	女厕所	Ladies
NAN CESUO	男厕所	Gentlemen
YUSHI	浴室	Bathroom
JIJIU	急救	First aid
YIYUAN	医院	Hospital
YAOFANG	药房	Dispensary
JINGCHAJU	警察局	Police
GONGANJU	公安局	Ministry of Public Security

XUEXIAO	学校	School
XIAOXUE	小学	Primary School
ZHONGHUE	中学	Secondary School
YUCHI	浴池	Public baths
LIFADIAN	理发店	Hairdresser
SHIWU ZHAOLING	失物招领	Lost property
XINGLI JICUNCHU	行李寄存处	Left luggage
XINGLIGUI	行李柜	Luggage lockers
YUYUE	预约	Reserved
YINGYE	营业	Open
TINGZHIYINGYE	停止营业	Closed
YINGYE SHIJIAN	营业时间	Opening hours
QUANMAN	全满	Sold out, full house
ZIZHU	自助	Self-service
SHOUKUAN TAI	收款台	Cash desk
BUXU XIYAN	不许吸烟	No smoking
YANJIN XIYAN	严禁吸烟	Smoking strictly prohibited
QING WU XI YAN	请勿吸烟	No smoking, please
KEYI XIYAN	可以吸烟	Smoking permitted
YINYONGSHUI	饮用水	Drinking water
FEI YINYONG SHUI	非饮用水	Not drinking water
WENXUN CHU	问询处	Information office
LOU/CENG	楼/层	Floor
YOU KONG FANG	有空房	Vacancies
SHOUPIAOCHU	售票处	Tickets
JIEDAISHI/ HOUCHESHI	接待室/候车室	Waiting room
YUETAI/ZHAN TAI	月台/站台	Platform
CAN CHE	餐车	Dining car
QICHE ZHAN	汽车站	Bus stop
GAOSU GONGLU	高速公路	Highway
WEIXIAN	危险	Danger
WEIXIAN DIDAI	危险地带	Dangerous bend
SHUANGXING XIAN	双行线	Two way traffic
QINZHI FANYUE	禁止翻越	Overtaking forbidden
QINZHI RUNEI	禁止入内	No entry
LUKOU	路口	Crossroads

YOUXING	右行	Keep right
CILU BUTONG	此路不通	No through traffic
DANXING LU	单行路	One way
MANXING	慢行	Slow
XIANSU	限速	Speed limit
JINZHI TINGCHE	禁止停车	No parking
TINGCHE CHANG	停车场	Car park
RAOXING	绕行	Diversion
HONGLÜ DENG	红绿灯	Traffic lights
QINGWU PANDENG	请勿攀登	No climbing
QING WU JIANTA CAOPING	请勿践踏草坪	Keep off the lawn
QING WU PAI ZHAO	请勿拍照	No photography
QING WU SUI DI TU TAN	请勿随地吐痰	No spitting
QING PAI DUI	请排队	Please queue
JINZHI DIAOYU	禁止钓鱼	No fishing
CHURU QING XIA CHE (cyclists entering guarded buildings)	出入请下车	Dismount at the gate
QING ZOU RENXING HENGDAO	请走人行横道	Cross at the pedestrian crossing
QING WU LUAN PAO GUOPI ZHIXIE	请勿乱抛果皮纸屑	No litter
YOUKE ZHI BU	游客止步	Stop here
QING WU CHUMO ZHANPIN	请勿触摸展品	Do not touch the exhibits
CUNBAO CHU/XIAO JIAN JI CUN CHU	存包处/小件寄存处	Bag deposit
CUN CHE CHU	存车处	Bicycle park
ZI XING CHE XIU LI BU	自行车修理部	Bicycle repairs
DA QI	打气	Air for bicycle tyres
JING/ANJING	静/安静	Silence
ANLING	按铃	Ring the bell

NUMBERS

Cardinal numbers

0	**líng** leeng ○
1	**yī** ee 一

[Note: yī is sometimes pronounced yào when speaking out high numbers e.g. one-one-four: yào yào sì.]

2	**èr** urr 二

[Note: Er and liang 两 both mean two. Follow the examples.]

3	**sān** san 三
4	**sì** si 四
5	**wǔ** woo 五
6	**liù** lyoo 六
7	**qī** chee 七
8	**bā** ba 八
9	**jiǔ** jew 九
10	**shí** shi 十
11	**shíyī** shi-ee 十一

12	**shíèr**
	shi-urr
	十二
13	**shísān**
	shi-san
	十三
14	**shísì**
	shi-si
	十四
15	**shíwǔ**
	shi-woo
	十五
16	**shíliù**
	shi-lyoo
	十六
17	**shíqī**
	shi-chee
	十七
18	**shíbā**
	shi-ba
	十八
19	**shíjiǔ**
	shi-jew
	十九
20	**èrshí**
	urr-shi
	二十
21	**èrshíyī**
	urr-shi-ee
	二十一
22	**èrshíèr**
	urr-shi-urr
	二十二
23	**èrshísān**
	urr-shi-san
	二十三
24	**èrshísì**
	urr-shi-si
	二十四
25	**èrshíwǔ**
	urr-shi-woo
	二十五
26	**èrshíliù**
	urr-shi-lyoo
	二十六

27	**èrshíqì**
	urr-shi-chee
	二十七
28	**èrshíbā**
	urr-shi-ba
	二十八
29	**èrshíjiǔ**
	urr-shi-jew
	二十九
30	**sānshí**
	san-shi
	三十

For numbers beyond 20 follow the pattern of ershi

31	**sānshíyī**
	san-shi-ee
	三十一
42	**sìshíèr**
	si-shi-urr
	四十二
43	**sìshísān**
	si-shi-san
	四十三
54	**wǔshísì**
	woo-shi-si
	五十四
65	**liùshíwǔ**
	lyoo-shi-woo
	六十五
76	**qīshíliù**
	chee-shi-lyoo
	七十六
87	**bāshíqī**
	ba-shi-chee
	八十七
98	**jiūshíbā**
	jew-shi-ba
	九十八
100	**yībǎi**
	ee-bigh
	一百
101	**yībǎi língyī**
	ee-bigh leeng-ee
	一百〇一

102	**yībǎi língèr**	
	ee-bigh leeng-urr	
	一百〇二	
125	**yībǎi èrshíwǔ**	
	ee-bigh urr-shi-woo	
	一百二十五	
150	**yībǎiwǔshí**	
	ee-bigh woo-shi	
	一百五十	
175	**yībǎi qīshíwǔ**	
	ee-bigh chee-shi-woo	
	一百七十五	
200	**èrbǎi**	
	urr-bigh	
	二百	
300	**sānbǎi**	
	san-bigh	
	三百	
400	**sìbǎi**	
	si-bigh	
	四百	
500	**wǔbǎi**	
	woo-bigh	
	五百	
600	**liùbǎi**	
	lyoo-bigh	
	六百	
1000	**yīqián**	
	ee-chyenn	
	一千	
1500	**yīqián wǔbǎi**	
	ee-chyenn woo-bigh	
	一千五百	
2000	**liǎngqián**	
	lyang-chyenn	
	两千	
5000	**wǔqián**	
	woo-chyenn	
	五千	
10,000	**yīwàn**	
	ee-wann	
	一万	
100,000	**shíwàn**	
	shi-wan	
	十万	

1,000,000	yībǎiwàn
	ee-bigh-wan
	一百万

Ordinal numbers

1st	dìyī
	dee-yee
	第一
2nd	dìèr
	dee-urr
	第二
3rd	dìsān
	dee-san
	第三
4th	dìsì
	dee-si
	第四
5th	dìwǔ
	dee-woo
	第五
6th	dìliù
	dee-lyoo
	第六
7th	dìqī
	dee-chee
	第七
8th	dìbā
	dee-ba
	第八
9th	dìjiǔ
	dee-jew
	第九
10th	dìshí
	dee-shi
	第十
11th	dìshíyī
	dee-shi-yee
	第十一
12th	dìshíèr
	dee-shi-urr
	第十二

TIME

What time is it?	**Xiànzài jǐdiǎn?** Syenn-dzigh jee-dyenn 现在几点?
It's one o'clock	**Yīdiǎn** Yee-dyenn 一点
It's two o'clock	**Liǎngdiǎn** Lyang-dyenn 二点
It's three o'clock	**Sāndiǎn** San-dyenn 三点
It's four o'clock	**Sìdiǎn** Si-dyenn 四点
in the morning	**shàngwǔ** (*at beginning of sentence*) shang-woo 上午
in the afternoon	**xiàwǔ** (*at beginning of sentence*) sya-woo 下午
in the evening	**wǎnshàng** (*at beginning of sentence*) wan-shang 晚上
in the night	**yèlǐ** (*at beginning of sentence*) ye-lee 夜里
It's 5 o'clock in the afternoon	**Xiànzài xiàwǔ wǔ diǎn** Syenn-dzigh sya-woo woo dyenn 现在下午五点
It's noon	**Xiànzài zhōngwǔle** Syenn-dzigh joong-woo-la 现在中午了
It's midnight	**Xiànzài bànyèle** Syenn-dzigh ban-yeh-la 现在半夜了
It's five past five	**Xiànzài wǔdiǎn wǔfēn** Syenn-dzigh woo-dyenn woo-fin 现在五点五分

It's ten past five

Xiànzài wǔdiǎn shífēn
Syenn-dzigh woo-dyenn shi-fin
现在五点十分

It's quarter past five

Xiànzài wǔdiǎn yīkè
Syenn-dzigh woo-dyenn ee-ko
现在五点一刻

It's twenty past five

Xiànzài wǔdiǎn èrshí
Syenn-dzigh woo-dyenn urr-shi
现在五点二十

It's twenty-five past five

Xiànzài wūdiǎn èrshíwǔ
Syenn-dzigh woo-dyenn urr-shi-
woo
现在五点二十五

It's half past five

Xiànzài wǔdiǎn bàn
Syenn-dzigh woo-dyenn ban
现在五点半

It's twenty-five to six

**Xiànzài chà èrshíwǔ fēn liù
diǎn**
Syenn-dzigh cha urr-shi-woo fin
lyoo dyenn
现在差二十五分六点

It's twenty to six

Xiànzài chà èrshífēn liù diǎn
Syenn-dzigh cha urr-shi-fin lyoo
dyenn
现在差二十分六点

It's a quarter to six

Xiànzài chà yī kè liù diǎn
Syenn-dzigh cha ee ko lyoo
dyenn
现在差一刻六点

It's ten to six

Xiànzài chà shífēn liù diǎn
Syenn-dzigh cha shi-fin lyoo
dyenn
现在差十分六点

It's five to six

Xiànzài chà wǔfēn liùdiǎn
Syenn-dzigh cha woo-fin lyoo-
dyenn
现在差五分六点

At what time does the train
leave?

Huǒ chē jǐdiǎn kāi?
Hwo-chuh jee-dyenn kigh
火车几点开?

At 1300 hours exactly

Shísāndiǎn zhèng
Shi-san-dyenn jung
十三点正

14.05	**Shísì diǎn líng wǔ fēn** Shi-sì dyenn leeng woo fin 十四点〇五分
15.10	**Shíwǔ diǎn shí fēn** Shi-woo dyenn shi fin 十五点十分
16.15	**Shíliù diǎn shíwǔ fēn** Shi-lyoo dyenn shi-woo fin 十六点十五分
17.20	**Shíqīdiǎn èrshífēn** Shi-chee-dyenn urr-shi-fin 十七点二十分
18.25	**Shíbā diǎn èrshíwǔ** Shi-ba dyenn urr-shi-woo 十八点二十五
19.30	**Shíqī diǎn sānshí** Shi-chee dyenn san-shi 十七点三十
20.35	**Èrshí diǎn sānshíwǔ** Urr-shi dyenn san-shi-woo 二十点三十五
21.40	**Èrshíyī diǎn sìshí** Urr-shi-yee dyenn si-shi 二十一点四十
22.45	**Èrshíèr diǎn sìshíwǔ** Urr-shi-urr dyenn si-shi-woo 二十二点四十五
23.50	**Èrshísān diǎn wǔshí** Urr-shi-san dyenn woo-shi 二十三点五十
0.55	**Líng wǔshíwǔ fēn** Ling woo-shi-woo fin 〇五十五分
in ten minutes	**Guò shífēnzhōng** Gwo shi-fin-joong 过十分钟
in a quarter of an hour	**Guò yīkèzhōng** Gwo yee-ko-joong 过一刻钟
in half an hour	**Guò bàn xiǎoshí** Gwo ban syaow-shir 过半小时

in three-quarters of an hour	**Guò sān kè zhōng**
	Gwo san ko joong
	过三刻钟

DAYS

Monday	**Xīngqīyī**
	Seeng-chee-yee
	星期一
Tuesday	**Xīngqīèr**
	Seeng-chee-urr
	星期二
Wednesday	**Xīngqīsān**
	Seeng-chee-san
	星期三
Thursday	**Xīngqīsì**
	Seeng-chee-si
	星期四
Friday	**Xīngqīwǔ**
	Seeng-chee-woo
	星期五
Saturday	**Xīngqīliù**
	Seeng-chee-lioo
	星期六
Sunday	**Xīngqītiān**
	Seeng-chee-tyenn
	星期天
last Monday	**shàng Xīngqīyī**
	shang Seeng-chee-yee
	上星期一
next Tuesday	**xià Xīngqīèr**
	sya Seeng-chee-urr
	下星期二
on Wednesday	**Xīngqīsān**
	Seeng-chee-san
	星期三
on Thursdays	**měi Xīngqīsì**
	may Seeng-chee-si
	每星期四
until Friday	**dào Xīngqīwǔ**
	daow Seeng-chee-woo
	到星期五
before Saturday	**zài Xīngqīliù yǐqián**
	dzigh Seeng-chee-lyoo ee-chyenn
	在星期六以前

after Sunday	**Xīngqītiān yǐhòu** Seeng-chee-tyenn yee-how 星期天以后
the day before yesterday	**qiántiān** chyenn-tyenn 前天
two days ago	**dà qiántiān** da chyenn-tyenn 大前天
yesterday	**zuótiān** dzo-tyenn 昨天
yesterday morning	**zuótiān shàngwǔ** dzo-tyenn shang-woo 昨天上午
yesterday afternoon	**zuótiān xiàwǔ** dzo-tyenn sya-woo 昨天下午
last night	**zuótiān wǎnshàng** dzo-tyenn wan-shang 昨天晚上
today	**jīntiān** jeen-tyenn 今天
this morning	**jīntiān zǎoshàng** jeen-tyenn dzao-shang 今天早上
this afternoon	**jīntiān xiàwǔ** jeen-tyenn sya-woo 今天下午
tonight	**jīntiān wǎnshàng** jeen-tyenn wan-shang 今天晚上
tomorrow	**míngtiān** meeng-tyenn 明天
tomorrow morning	**míngtiān shàngwǔ** meeng-tyenn shang-woo 明天上午
tomorrow afternoon	**míngtiān xiàwǔ** meeng-tyenn sya-woo 明天下午
tomorrow evening	**míngtiān wǎnshàng** meeng-tyenn wan-shang 明天晚下

tomorrow night	**míngtiān yèlǐ** meeng-tyenn ye-lee 明天夜里
the day after tomorrow	**hòutiān** how-tyenn 后天
in two days' time	**dà hòutiān** da how-tyenn 大后天

MONTHS AND DATES

January	**Yīyuè** Ee-yweh 一月
February	**Èryuè** Urr-yweh 二月
March	**Sānyuè** San-yweh 三月
April	**Sìyuè** Si-yweh 四月
May	**Wǔyuè** Woo-yweh 五月
June	**Liùyuè** Lyoo-yweh 六月
July	**Qīyuè** Chee-yweh 七月
August	**Bāyuè** Ba-yweh 八月
September	**Jiǔyuè** Jew-yweh 九月
October	**Shíyuè** Shi-yweh 十月

November	**Shíyī yuè** Shi-yee yweh 十一月
December	**Shíèr yuè** Shi-urr-yweh 十二月
in January	**Yīyuè dāngzhōng** Yee-yweh dang-joong 一月当中
until February	**yīzhí dao Èryuè** yee-jih daow Urr-yweh 一直到二月
before March	**Zài Sānyuè yǐqián** Dzigh San-yweh ee-chyenn 在三月以前
after April	**Sìyuè yǐhòu** Si-yweh yee-how 四月以后
during May	**Wǔyuè dāngzhōng** Woo-yweh dang-joong 五月当中
not until June	**bù néng zài Liùyuè yǐqián** boo nung dzigh Lyoo-yweh ee- chyenn 不能在六月以前
the beginning of June	**Liùyuè chū** Lyoo-yweh choo 六月初
the middle of August	**Bāyuè zhōngqī** Ba-yweh joong-chee 八月中期
the end of September	**Jiǔyuè dǐ** Jew-yweh dee 九月底
last month	**shàngge yuè** shang-ga yweh 上个月
this month	**zhèige yuè** jay-ga yweh 这个月
next month	**xiàge yuè** sya-ga yweh 下个月

in spring	**chūntiān**	
	choon-tyenn	
	春天	
in summer	**xiàtiān**	
	sya-tyenn	
	夏天	
in autumn	**qiūtiān**	
	chyoo-tyenn	
	秋天	
in winter	**dōngtiān**	
	doong-tyenn	
	冬天	
this year	**jīnnián**	
	jeen-nyenn	
	今年	
last year	**qùnián**	
	choo-nyenn	
	去年	
next year	**míngnián**	
	ming-nyenn	
	明年	
in 1990	**yījiǔ jiǔlíng nián**	
	yee-jew jew-ling nyenn	
	一九九〇年	
in 1993	**yījiǔ jiǔsān nián**	
	yee-jew jew-san nyenn	
	一九九三年	
in 1997	**yījiǔ jiǔqī nián**	
	yee-jew jew-chee nyenn	
	一九九七年	
What's the date today?	**Jīntiān shì jǐyuè jǐrì?**	
	Jeen-tyenn shi jee-yweh jee-ri	
	今天是几月几日?	
What day (of the week) is it today?	**Jīntiān shì xīngqījǐ?**	
	Jeentyenn shi seeng-chee jee	
	今天是星期几?	
It's the first	**Shì yīrì**	
	Shi yee-ri	
	是一日	
It's the second	**Shì èrrì**	
	Shi urr-ri	
	是二日	

It's the third	**Shì sānrì** Shi san-ri 是三日
It's the fourth [*For numbers see p.128*]	**Shì sìrì** Shi si-ri 是四日
It's the 6th of March	**Sānyuè liùrì** San-yweh lyoo-ri 三月六日
It's the 12th of April	**Sìyuè shíèr rì** Si-yweh shi-urr ri 四月十二日
It's the 21st of August	**Bāyuè èrshíyī rì** Ba-yweh urr-shi-yee ri 八月二十一日

Public holidays

On these days, offices and schools are closed:

1 January	Yuándàn (New Year's Day) 元旦
late January/early February	Chūnjié (Spring Festival) 春节
1 May	Guójì Láodòng jié (Labour Day) 国际劳动节
1 October	Guóqìngjié (National Day) 国庆节

Other holidays, following China's traditional calendar, fall mainly according to lunar dates. These are festivals rather than holidays, observed more in some parts of the country than others and in Chinese communities outside China often more than in mainland China.

Yuánxiāo	元宵	Lantern festival, 15th day of the first lunar month
Qīngmíng	清明	Grave-sweeping, 4-5 April
Duānwǔ	端午	Dragon boat festival, 5th of the 5th lunar month
Zhōngqiū	中秋	Mid-Autumn, 15th of the 8th lunar month

The following socialist/communist festivals are marked in China:

8 March	三八节	International Women's Day
1 June	六一节	Children's Day
1 August	八一节	Army Day

COUNTRIES AND NATIONALITIES

Countries

Australia	**Àodàlìyà** Ow-da-lee-ya 澳大利亚
Austria	**Àodìlì** Ow-dee-lee 澳地利
Belgium	**Bǐlìshí** Bee-lee-shi 比利时
Canada	**Jiānádà** Jya-na-da 加拿大
China	**Zhōngguó** Joong-guo 中国
England	**Yīngguó** Eeng-gwo 英国
Germany	**Déguó** Duh-gwo 德国
Greece	**Xīlà** See-la 希腊
India	**Yìndù** Een-doo 印度
Japan	**Rìběn** Ri-ben 日本
Korea	**Cháoxiān** Chaow-syenn 朝鲜
Italy	**Yìdàlì** Ee-da-lee 意大利
Netherlands	**Hélán** Ho-lan 荷兰

New Zealand	**Xīn Xīlán** Seen See-lan 新西兰
Northern Ireland	**Běi Àiěrlán** Bay Aye-urr-lan 北爱尔兰
Pakistan	**Bājisīdǎn** Ba-jee-si-dan 巴基斯坦
Portugal	**Pútáoyá** Poo-taow-ya 葡萄牙
Scotland	**Sūgélán** Soo-gu-lan 苏格兰
Spain	**Xībānyá** See-ban-ya 西
Soviet Union	**Sūlián** Soo-lyenn 苏联
Switzerland	**Ruìshì** Rway-shih 瑞士
United States	**Měiguó** May-gwo 美国
Wales	**Wēiěrsī** Way-urr-s 威尔斯

The provinces of China

Three cities are administratively separate

BĚIJĪNG	北京	also known as Peking
TIĀNJĪN	天津	also known as Tientsin
SHÀNGHǍI	上海	

Several 'autonomous regions' with largely non-Han-Chinese populations line the western borders. See map, pp.12 and 13.

AUTONOMOUS REGIONS	自治区	**ZÌZHÌQŪ**
Xinjiang Uighur		**Xīnjiāng Wéiwúěrzú**
		Seen-jyang Way-woo-urr-dzoo
		新疆维吾尔族
Tibet		**Xīzàng**
		See-dzang
		西藏
Ningxia Hui		**Níngxià Huízú**
		Ning-sya Hway-dzoo
		宁夏回族
Inner Mongolia		**Nèi Měnggǔ**
		Nay Mung-goo
		内蒙古
Guǎngxī Zhuang		**Guǎngxī Zhuàngzú**
		Gwang-see Jwang-dzoo
		广西壮族

PROVINCES	省	**SHENG**
Hēilóngjiāng	黑龙江	Hay-long-jyang
Jílín	吉林	Jee-lin
Liáoníng	辽宁	Lyaow-neeng
Gānsù	甘肃	Gan-soo
Qīnghǎi	青海	Cheeng-high
Shǎnxī	陕西	Shan-see (third tone)
Shānxi	山西	Shan-see (first tone)
Héběi	河北	Ho-bay
Shāndōng	山东	Shandoong
Hénán	河南	Ho-nan
Húběi	湖北	Hoo-bay
Húnán	湖南	Hoo-nan
Jiāngxī	江西	Jyang-see
Guìzhōu	贵洲	Gway-jow
Sìchuān	四川	Ssi-chwan
Jiāngsū	江苏	Jyang-soo
Zhèjiāng	浙江	Juh-jyang
Ānhūi	安徽	An-hway
Fújiàn	福建	Foo-jyenn
Guǎngdōng	广东	Gwang-doong
Yúnnán	云南	Yoon-nan
Táiwān	台湾	Tigh-wan

NATIONALITIES/PROVINCIAL ORIGINS

To make a person from a place-name, just add the word for 'person' 人 'rén' to the country or province or city. The same word is used for an American, some Americans, male(s) or female(s): they are called 'Meiguoren 美国人 '.

Yīngguó rén 英国人	An Englishman/woman
Sìchuān rén 四川人	A Sichuanese
Běijīng rén 北京人	A Beijinger
Shànghǎi rén 上海人	A Shanghainese
Nǐ shì Měiguórén ma? 你是美国人吗?	Are you American?
Wǒ shì Húnán rén 我是湖南人	I am from Hunan

[Note: Mainland China calls itself Zhonghua renmin gongheguo 中华人民共和国 , the People's Republic of China. Taiwan, seat of the Nationalist government-in-exile, calls itself Zhonghua Minguo 中华民国 , the Republic of China. Both regimes claim to be the only legitimate ruler of all China, although the Nationalists were defeated in 1949 and have not held real power since then in mainland China.]

DEPARTMENT STORE GUIDE

Nǚzhuāngbù	女装部	Ladies' clothes
Nánzhuāngbù	男装部	Men's clothes
Chuángshàng yòngpǐn	床上用品	Bed linen
Tóngzhuāngbù	童装部	Children's clothes
Tǐyù yòngpǐn	体育用品	Sports goods
Rìyòng bǎihuò	日用百货	Haberdashery
Huàzhuāngpǐn	化装品	Cosmetics
Xiémàobù	鞋帽部	Shoes, hats
Wénhuà yòngpǐn	文化用品	Stationery
Jiāyòng diànqì	家用电器	Household and electrical
Shǒushìbù	首饰部	Jewellery
Fǎngzhīpǐn	纺织品	Fabrics
Zhàoxiàng qìcái	照相器材	Photographic
Píhuòbù	皮货部	Leather goods
Shōukuǎntái	收款台	Till, checkout
Jiājù	家具	Furniture
Chúfángyòngjù	厨房用具	Kitchen goods
Yānjiǔbù	烟酒部	Wines, tobacco
Chènyī	衬衣	Shirts
Wánjù	玩具	Toys
Máoxiàn	毛线	Knitting wool
Shízhuāng	时装	Young fashions
Zhōngbiǎobù	钟表部	Watches and clocks
Cíqì	磁器	Porcelain
Tètǐfúzhuāng	特体服装	Outsize
Dìtǎn	地毯	Carpets
Chuānglián	窗帘	Curtains
Bōli	玻璃	Glass
Gǔwù	古物	Antiques
Huàláng	画廊	Paintings

CLOTHING SIZES

Clothes are measured in European, British or American sizes. Use
公分 gōngfēn for centimetres and 英寸 Yīngcùn for inches.
Remember – always try on clothes before buying. Clothing sizes
are usually unreliable.

women's dresses and suits

Europe	38	40	42	44	46	48
UK	32	34	36	38	40	42
USA	10	12	14	16	18	20

men's suits and coats

Europe	46	48	50	52	54	56
UK and USA	36	38	40	42	44	46

men's shirts

Europe	36	37	38	39	41	42	43
UK and USA	14	14½	15	15½	16	16½	17

socks

Chinese	38-39	39-40	40-41	41-42	42-43
UK and USA	9½	10	10½	11	11½

shoes

Chinese	34	35½	36½	38	39	41	42	43	44	45
UK	2	3	4	5	6	7	8	9	10	11
USA	3½	4½	5½	6½	7½	8½	9½	10½	11½	12½

Do it yourself

Some notes on the language

- There is no word for 'the' in Chinese. Most Chinese nouns do not tell if they are 'the man', 'a man', 'the men' or 'some men'. Often, my, your and his/her are also left out in situations where English speakers would expect to use them. What Chinese does have is 'measure words' used when the word for 'a/an' (which is the same as the word for 'one') is used. Measure words are also used between any number and the noun it refers to.
  Chinese words do not indicate gender (masculine or feminine endings).

The apple	pǐngguǒ	苹果
The address	dìzhǐ	地址
The bus ticket	chēpiào	车票
a cup of tea	yībēi chá	一杯茶
a glass of wine	yībēijiǔ	一杯酒
the key	yàoshí	钥匙
the luggage	xíngli	行李
the menu	càidān	菜单
the newspaper	bàozhǐ	报纸
the receipt	shōujù	收据
the sandwich	sānmíngzhì	三明治
the suitcase	shǒutíbāo	手提包
the telephone directory	diànhuàbú	电话簿

Important things to remember

- The most common measure word is 'ge' 个. Use it if you don't know the correct measure word for what you want to say:

A room	yīge fángzi	一个房子
A notebook	yīge běnzi	一个本子
An American	yīge Měiguó rén	一个美国人
five apples	wǔge pǐngguǒ	五个苹果

- Remember you must put a measure word between a number and its noun.

| The newspaper | bàozhǐ |
| three newspapers | sānge bàozhǐ |

- Special measure words are used for:

a book	yī *běn* shū (one volume book)	一本书
a pen	yī*zhī* bī (one stick pen)	一枝笔
a yuan (Chinese dollar)	yī *kuài* qián (one piece money)	一块钱
a sheet of paper	yī *zhang* zhǐ	一张纸

- Most of the time there is no need to indicate if you are talking about one or several things:

table(s)	zhuōzi	桌子
bicycle(s)	zìxíng chē	自行车
taxi(s)	chūzū qìchē	出租汽车

- A few words, usually describing groups of people, add on a suffix 'men' to show that they are plural:

	Singular	Plural	
student/s	xuésheng	xuéshengmen	学生们
child/ren	háizi	háizimen	孩子们
comrade/s	tóngzhì	tóngzhìmen	同志们
friend/s	péngyou	péngyoumen	朋友们
gentleman/men	xiānsheng	xiānshengmen	先生们

- Practise saying these sentences in Chinese:

I'll buy an apple (No word for 'I' or 'a' needed)	Mǎi píngguǒ	买苹果
I'll buy a newspaper	Wǒ mǎi bàozhǐ	我买报纸
I'll buy a sandwich	Wǒ mǎi sānmíngzhì	我买三明治
Give me two beers	Gěi wǒ liǎngge píjiǔ	给我两个啤酒
Give me one apple		
Give me five sandwiches		

- It can be helpful to think of measures of what you want, e.g. one bowl rice, one bottle wine, one pack of cigarettes, to help you get the hang of Chinese measure words.

| I'd like a bowl of rice | **Wǒ xiǎngyào yīwǎn mǐfàn**
我想要一碗米饭 |
| I'd like a bottle of wine | **Wǒ xiǎngyào yīpíng pútao jiǔ**
我想要一瓶葡萄酒 |

- Some and any, like a and the, don't need to trouble you in Chinese.

Do you have some coffee?	**Yǒu kāfēi ma?** 有咖啡吗?
Do you have some water?	**(shuǐ)**
Do you have some chocolate?	**(qiǎo kē lì)**
I'd like some apples	**Wǒ xiǎngyào píngguǒ** 我想要苹果
I'd like some Western food	**Wǒ xiǎngyào Xī cài** 我想要西菜
I'd like some chicken noodles	**Wǒ xiǎngyào jīsì chǎomiàn** 我想要鸡丝炒面
Is there any lemonade?	**Yǒu qìshuǐ ma?** 有汽水吗?
Is there any beer?	**(píjiǔ)**
Is there any mineral water?	**(kuàngquánshuǐ)**
Where can I get some yoghurt?	**Nǎli yǒu suān niú nǎi?** 哪里有酸牛奶
Where can I get some fruit?	**(shuǐguǒ)**
Where can I get some coffee?	**(kāfēi)**
I'll have some beer	**Yào píjiǔ** 要啤酒
I'll have some tea	**(green tea: lǜchá)** **(black tea: hóngchá)**
Have you got the key?	**Yǒu yàoshí ma?** 有钥匙吗?
Have you got the timetable?	**Yǒu shíkebiao ma?**
Have you got the menu?	**Yǒu càidān ma?**
Have you got the receipt?	**Yǒu shōujù ma?**
Where is the key?	**Yàoshí zài nǎr?** 钥匙在哪儿?
Where is the timetable?	**Shíkèbiǎo zài nǎr?**

Now try making up some more sentences along the same lines.
Try adding 'please tell me' 'Qǐngwèn' at the beginning.

MY/YOUR et cetera

To show ownership, use the words below:

My book	**wǒde shū** 我的书
Your book	**nǐde shū** 你的书
his/her book	**tāde shū** 他的书

our book	**wǒmen de shū** 我们的书
your book	**nǐmen de shū** 你们的书
their book	**tāmen de shū** 他们的书

The word 'de' 的 always shows a connection or ownership.
It comes either between an adjective and a noun:

clever students	**cóngmíng de xuésheng**
a good restaurant	**hǎo de fànguǎnr**
nice music	**hǎoting de yīnyuè**

or to show ownership (possessive indicator)

Mr Wang's room	**Wáng xiānsheng de fángzi**
the child's clothes	**hǎizi de yīfu**
the interpreter's name	**fànyi de míngzi**

THIS AND THAT

This	**Zhèige** 这个
That	**Nèige or Nàge** **(Use either)** 那个

You can use zhei and nei (this and that) with the most common
measure word 'ge'.

What is that?	**Nèi shi shénme?** 那是什么?
I want that	**Wǒ yào nèige** 我要那个
This child	**Zhèige hǎizi** 这个孩子
That train	**Nèige huǒchē** 那个火车

'This' and 'That' are like numbers. They need a measure word like
'ge' between them and the word they are joined to.

QUESTIONS

There are two ways to ask questions. Look at these examples.

He is buying a ticket.	**Tā mǎi piào.**
Is he buying a ticket?	**Tā *mǎi* piaò *ma?***
	or
	Tā *mǎi bu mǎi* piào?
She loves China.	**Tā *ài* Zhōngguó**
Does she love China?	**Tā *ài* Zhōngguó *ma?***
	Tā *ài bù ài* Zhōnggúo?

Either add the question word *ma* to the end of your sentence
or repeat the verb in the form
buy not buy
love not love
Remember that the word for 'not' is bu 不, except with the word
'have/there is' yǒu 有.

So you often hear the question:

Yǒuméi yǒu	meaning 'do you have any'
有没有	'is there any'

for example Nǐmen zhèr *yǒu méi yǒu* Yīngwén bàozhǐ?
Do you have any English-language newspapers?
Shànghǎi *yǒu méi yǒu* dòngwùyuán?
Is there a zoo in Shanghai?

Practise asking 'is there any' with the list of nouns on p.73

Of course there are common question words too:

Shéi	Who?	谁
Shénme	What?	什么
Shénme shíhou	When?	什么时候
Zěnme	How?	怎么
Nǎr	Where?	哪儿

Shéi hē píjiǔ?	Who is drinking beer?
Zhèi shì shénme?	(Literally: this is what?)
Shénme shíhou dào Shànghǎi?	(When do we get to Shanghai?)
Dào Běijīng Fàndiàn zěnme zǒu?	(How do I get to the Peking Hotel?)
Yǒuyì Shāngdiàn zài nǎr?	(Literally: Friendship Store is where?)

Notice that the sentence order is different from ours in English.
The way to learn is to listen to examples and look at the questions
in the book.

Practise making sentences with ... zài nǎr?, using the list of places on pages 119 and 120.

HELPING OTHERS

You have learned how to help yourself by using phrases like:

I'd like a beer	Xiǎngyào yīge píjiǔ
Where can I get a map?	Nǎr yǒu dìtú?
I want some chocolate	Yào qiǎokelì
I need a receipt	Xūyào shōujù

Since Chinese usually omits the subject of the sentence, these same phrases will enable you to help one or more English speakers having trouble making themselves understood. Just point to them and the Chinese audience will understand who the request is for.

It is not necessary to say the words for he, she or they in Chinese unless you want to be terribly emphatic - 'It's he who wants the taxi.' 'Tā yào chūzūqìchē.' The word for 'he' Tā 他 is pronounced the same as the word for 'she' Tā 她. Notice that the characters are different. He (tā 他) is written with the man radical 人 and she (tā 她) is written with the woman radical 女. You may have noticed that many Chinese people muddle 'he' and 'she' when speaking English. Now you know why.

Verbs in Chinese don't change with person or tense.

Wǒ chī	I eat, I ate, I will eat
Tā chī	He eats, he ate, he will eat
Tāmen chī	They eat, they ate, they will eat

This makes it easy for a few phrases to help you in many different situations – make yourself understood by combining the phrases you have learned with pointing and using a dictionary.

MORE PRACTICE

Try to learn the sounds of Chinese as well as you can.
The phonetic alphabet pinyin is used throughout China and in Singapore. Most newspapers and broadcasting organizations in the West now use pinyin to romanize Chinese names, so you see:

Mao Zedong	and not Mao Tse-tung
Zhou Enlai	and not Chou En-lai
Suzhou	and not Soochow
and so on	

Some familiar names are becoming better known in their pinyin versions. China's capital, Beijing, used to be known as Peking, but nowadays both versions are familiar. Other identity confusions are:

Guangzhou	same as Canton
Xi'an	same as Sian
Chongqing	same as Chungking
Nanjing	same as Nanking

Watch out also for names which you have heard in their Cantonese versions:

CANTONESE	STANDARD CHINESE
Hong Kong	Xiang gang
dimsum (dumplings)	dianxin
Sun Yat-sen	Sun Zhongshan
Chiang Kai-shek	Jiang Jieshi

The dynasties of China's past are also known both in old-style romanization and in pinyin.

PINYIN	OLD-STYLE
Qin 221-206 BC	Ch'in
Han (206 BC-221 AD)	
Tang (618-907)	T'ang
Song (960-1278)	Sung
Yuan (1206-1333)	
Ming (1368-1644)	
Qing (1644-1911)	Ch'ing
Republic (1911-1949)	
People's Republic (1949-	

Useful reading

Before travelling to China, find a good guidebook.

We recommend the Passport Books China Guide Series, which includes separate books on **All China; Beijing; Fujian; Guilin, Canton & Guangdong; Hangzhou & Zhejiang; Nanjing & Jiangsu; Shanghai; The Silk Road; Tibet; Xi'an; The Yangzi River; Yunnan.**

Index

FOREIGN LANGUAGE BOOKS

Multilingual
The Insult Dictionary:
How to Give 'Em Hell in 5 Nasty
Languages
The Lover's Dictionary:
How to be Amorous in 5 Delectable
Languages
Multilingual Phrase Book
Let's Drive Europe Phrasebook
CD-ROM "Languages of the World":
Multilingual Dictionary Database

Spanish
Vox Spanish and English Dictionaries
NTC's Dictionary of Spanish False Cognates
Nice 'n Easy Spanish Grammar
Spanish Verbs and Essentials of Grammar
Getting Started in Spanish
Spanish à la Cartoon
Guide to Spanish Idioms
Guide to Correspondence in Spanish
The Hispanic Way

French
NTC's New College French and English
Dictionary
French Verbs and Essentials of Grammar
Real French
Getting Started in French
Guide to French Idioms
Guide to Correspondence in French
French à la Cartoon
Nice 'n Easy French Grammar
NTC's Dictionary of *Faux Amis*
NTC's Dictionary of Canadian French
Au courant: Expressions for Communicating in
Everyday French

German
Schöffler-Weis German and English Dictionary
Klett German and English Dictionary
Getting Started in German
German Verbs and Essentials of Grammar
Guide to German Idioms
Street-wise German
Nice 'n Easy German Grammar
German à la Cartoon
NTC's Dictionary of German False Cognates

Italian
Zanichelli Super-Mini Italian and English
Dictionary
Zanichelli New College Italian and English
Dictionary
Getting Started in Italian
Italian Verbs and Essentials of Grammar

Greek
NTC's New College Greek and English
Dictionary

Latin
Essentials of Latin Grammar

Hebrew
Everyday Hebrew

Chinese
Easy Chinese Phrasebook and Dictionary

Korean
Korean in Plain English

Polish
The Wiedza Powszechna Compact Polish and
English Dictionary

Swedish
Swedish Verbs and Essentials of Grammar

Russian
Complete Handbook of Russian Verbs
Essentials of Russian Grammar
Business Russian
Basic Structure Practice in Russian

Japanese
Easy Kana Workbook
Easy Hiragana
Easy Katakana
101 Japanese Idioms
Japanese in Plain English
Everyday Japanese
Japanese for Children
Japanese Cultural Encounters
Nissan's Business Japanese

"Just Enough" Phrase Books
Chinese, Dutch, French, German, Greek,
Hebrew, Hungarian, Italian, Japanese,
Portuguese, Russian, Scandinavian,
Serbo-Croat, Spanish
Business French, Business German, Business
Spanish

Audio and Video Language Programs
Just Listen 'n Learn Spanish, French,
German, Italian, Greek, and Arabic
Just Listen 'n Learn...Spanish,
French, German PLUS
Conversational...Spanish, French, German,
Italian, Russian, Greek, Japanese, Thai,
Portuguese in 7 Days
Practice & Improve Your...Spanish, French,
Italian, and German
Practice & Improve Your...Spanish, French,
Italian, and German PLUS
Improve Your...Spanish, French, Italian, and
German: The P&I Method
VideoPassport French
VideoPassport Spanish
How to Pronounce...Spanish, French,
German, Italian, Russian, Japanese
Correctly

PASSPORT BOOKS
a division of *NTC Publishing Group*
Lincolnwood, Illinois USA